W9-CCW-328

THE MUST OF THE SECOND BIRTH

Robert G. Lee

THE MUST OF THE SECOND BIRTH

And Other Sermons

Fleming H. Revell Company

Library of Congress Catalog Card Number: 60–5499

Printed in the United States of America

1.1

Acknowledgment is made to the following, who have granted permission for the reprinting of copyrighted material:

APPLETON-CENTURY-CROFTS, INC. and *Century Magazine* for excerpt from "Cenotaph of Lincoln" by James T. McKay.

BOBBS-MERRILL COMPANY, INC. for "Let Something Good Be Said" by James Whitcomb Riley, from *Home-Folks*.

Contents

THE MUST OF THE SECOND BIRTH

1 Preaching the Cross

> *For the preaching of the cross is to them that perish foolishness; but unto us which are saved it is the power of God* (I Corinthians 1:18).
> *Him, being delivered by the determinate counsel and foreknowledge of God, ye have taken, and by wicked hands have crucified and slain* (Acts 2:23).

There has been and *must* be:

I. PREACHING.

Talmage, playing on a gospel harp of one thousand strings, preached the cross.

Spurgeon, with voice eloquent with spiritual passion, preached the cross.

Whitefield, riding the country over, crossing the ocean many times, preaching on land and sea, preached the cross.

Jonathan Edwards, throwing revival torches everywhere, preached the cross.

Moody, taking one continent in one hand and another continent in another hand and rocking them both toward God, preached the cross.

Wesley, carrying his proclamation on winds of flame to every part of his native land, preached the cross.

Truett, opening fountains of penitential tears with wooing preaching, preached the cross.

Carroll, theological juggernaut, crushing opponents of truth with mighty preaching, preached the cross.

Dement, as gentle as dew on flowers, preached the cross.

Joe Parker, preaching till men became unaware of their surroundings, preached the cross.

Robert Hall, in his most impassioned moods drawing men out of their seats, preached the cross.

Christmas Evans stirring the land as when a storm hits it, preached the cross.

William Carey, preaching with pen and word of mouth, opening the blind alleys of ignorance into endless highways of wisdom for millions of people, preached the cross.

Adoniram Judson transformed the blighted wilderness into a garden, uprooted the thorn tree, and planted the cedars of God by preaching the cross.

Paul, who compassed the earth with the truths of redemption, believed that the first and weightiest truth of Christianity was the death of Christ—not in a bed by nurses and doctors attended, but on the cross for our sins. To him, as it should be to us, Christ's cross-death was the keystone of the arch, the cornerstone of the temple of truth, the universal symbol and unmistakable message of Christianity.

In the New Testament, Christ's crucifixion is mentioned in every book except in three short Epistles: Philemon, II John, III John.

Matthew, not to mention many passages where Christ's

death is foretold, writes of the crucifixion in two long chapters
of 141 verses.

Mark, who records the *works* of Jesus more than the *words*
of Jesus, gives 116 verses to the crucifixion.

Luke, writing by the Holy Spirit, as a physician and in love
with the Great Physician, whom he had not seen, devotes two
long chapters to describing the arrest and crucifixion.

John, fiery in his zeal, writer of the fourth Gospel, three
Epistles and Revelation, his name being the last name of man
to appear in the Bible, uses about one half of his Gospel to
deal with events close to the end.

In Acts—what do we find? All the preceding centers in the
death and resurrection of Jesus Christ.

Peter at Pentecost, spoke of Jesus "delivered by the determinate counsel and foreknowledge of God"—crucified and
slain by the band of lawless men.

Peter in the temple spoke to the people of how they "killed
the Prince of Life" having as his theme "Jesus Christ of Nazareth whom ye crucified" (Acts 4:10).

The accused apostles spoke of "Jesus whom ye slew and
hanged on a tree" (Acts 5:30).

Cornelius was told of Jesus whom they slew, hanging him
on a tree, "Him God raised up the third day" (Acts 10:40).

Again Paul, at Antioch, speaks of Jesus suffering unto death
under Pontius Pilate (Acts 13:28–29).

Paul, at Thessalonica, reasoned from the Old Testament
Scriptures "that it behoved Christ to suffer" (Luke 24:46;
Acts 17:13).

Paul, at Athens, the intellectual center of the world,
preached the death and resurrection of Jesus (Acts 17:31).

Paul, at Corinth, "determined not to know anything among you, save Jesus Christ, and him crucified" (I Corinthians 2:2).

Paul, writing to the church at Galatia, spoke of how Jesus "gave himself for our sins" (Galatians 1:4), and then, with righteous indignation, he wrote as though with a flash of lightning: "But though we, or an angel from heaven, preach any other gospel unto you than that which we have preached unto you, let him be accursed" (Galatians 1:8).

Then Paul showed how he believed that the cross is supreme and crucial—to God, to man, to the enemies. He believed, as should every one of us, that the cross is the center of the universe and of history.

Peter was looking toward the cross and listening to the dripping of sinless blood when he wrote: "Who his own self bare our sins in his own body on the tree, that we, being dead to sins, should live unto righteousness: by whose stripes ye were healed" (I Peter 2:24).

And John was seeing Calvary when he wrote: "Jesus Christ, who is the faithful witness, and the first begotten of the dead, and the prince of the kings of the earth. Unto him that loved us, and washed us from our sins in his own blood . . . be glory and dominion for ever and ever. Amen" (Revelation 1:5, 6).

To take the cross out of our preaching—whether that preaching be in tent or crude tabernacle or the isolated church up the creek or the country church or the big church in the city—is like taking heat out of fire, melody out of music, numbers out of mathematics, fact out of history, mind out of metaphysics, words out of vocabularies.

The cross stands at the center of human history and human progress. To the cross all history converges; from the cross all real progress proceeds. The cross, in centuries past even as in our day, has freed the hearts of men from sin, has broken the shackles of the consciences of men, has introduced to the world the true conception of the dignity of men, has changed savages into tenderhearted servants of God, has exalted the sense of honor, justice, and righteousness in the hearts of men everywhere, has multiplied the Twelve who loved God into millions who love God. All science, all progress, all knowledge, all government can wisely and appropriately place flowers at the foot of the cross and glory on its head.

The preaching of the cross, for us, is amid today's appalling

II. PERVERSITIES.

Today black snow falls.

The fever of life's fierce heat burns all divine dew off the grass. Spiritual mercury in many schools and churches has fallen low. Critical Philistines of transcendent cleverness submit the warm wonder of Christianity to cold and merciless analysis. Faith's wings are clipped by Reason's scissors—creating tragedy worse than when Samson was shorn by Delilah's shears.

Fat deformities would, if they could, force us to substitute for Christianity's vital bread a chunk of cloud bank buttered with the night wind. Intellectuals, unaware of the rattle of the dry bones of their conceit, whose minds have a superficial mental illumination that lacks the urge of sacrificial passion, have sought to bring about an intellectual recoil against any emotional expression whatsoever. Spiritual latitudes are as wide as the Sahara Desert and correspondingly dry.

The Bible is summoned to appear at the bar of human reason—as Liberals whack at the supernatural, going nowhere so fast they arrive out of breath, talking more and more of less and less. And some churches, victims of lethargy and red-blooded convictions, have become "drifting sepulchres, manned by frozen crews," while many Christians, living in luxury, are like flowers frostbitten, like citrus groves frozen into practical worthlessness.

And many, forgetting that "the school is a stage in process," live and move under the illusion that the theological school can provide the future minister with all the mental, moral, and spiritual equipment he will need before he enters the pastorate, about which some seminary professors know little—really.

Today, few righteously angry voices challenge this era of passiveness. So much is this true that Dr. Herbert Merza—his voice carrying the pain of his heart—asks:

Is there no Victor Hugo to challenge men to great action? Where is the Patrick Henry to debate against tyranny? And the Martin Luthers to speak the clear voice of God? Is there no one to emulate Jesus and rid the temple of money changers? Where are God's angry men?

We live at a time when good men have become men dangerous to the welfare of the church because they are chronic absentees from the main job.

Today, seeing Hydra-headed evils all around us, having many who "loose wild tongues that hold not God in awe," we have sympathy for him who wrote (whether in cynicism or lamentation, I know not) these words:

> I vow, O God,
> Not for all Thy power furled and unfurled,
> Nor for all the temples to Thy Glory built
> Would I assume the ignominious guilt
> Of having made such men in such a world.

We live at a time when many, who are supposed to preach the Word, speak of hell as "only the wild nightmare of a dis-

ordered brain" and of heaven as a place being "a sickly senti-
mentality"—giving forth sermonettes that are like "just swing-
ing on the garden gate," instead of coming down into the lives
of men with pertinent meaning.

Today, looking at our nation, we know that if our creditors
would foreclose, insolvency and bankruptcy would face the nation. And the President, in recent months, signed a new law
—lifting the debt ceiling so that we can go deeper into the dark
dungeon of insolvency.

And today, communism, with its perpetual rule of terror,
wherein hate is elevated to a virtue and becomes a primary instrument of social policy—wherein individual men are ex-
pendable even to the extent that mass murder is permissible
whenever necessary to the seizure or retention of political
power, wherein the universe and all of life are subject to the
workings of an insensate dialectical materialism—this curse of
the earth in antithesis to the principles incorporated in the life
and words of Jesus "makes communism to stand revealed as
Antichrist."

All these realities—and more—makes a holy and insistent
imperative:

III. PROCLAMATION OF THE CROSS BY LIP AND LIFE.

We are to preach the cross, not submit it for subdued discus-
sion in the academic grove. Not with piping voice, but with
trumpet tones that offer no uncertain sound.

Not as epicures in philosophies. Not as feeders of inflamed
popular appetite, for amusement. Not as administrators of laugh-
ing gas for the painless extraction of sin. Not as dainty tasters
of intellectual subtleties. Not as experts in speculative cleverness. Not as declarers of the airy abstractions of an "up-to-date"

gospel. Not as dealers in fine-spun, metaphysical disquisitions. Not as those afflicted with faltering tongues. Not as those cursed with faint hearts. Not with the mere exhortations of moralists.

But with wooing and warning urgency that lifts up the crucified Christ and warns men that "the wrath of God is revealed from heaven against all ungodliness and unrighteousness of men who hold the truth in unrighteousness" (Romans 1:18).

We must believe and preach and get others to believe that the cross is the great centrality in all true worship, in all daring missionary enterprise, in all genuinely sacrificial giving, in all crucifiedly consecrated living, in all pulpits that are not extinct volcanoes where no fire is.

And we must preach the cross, a goal in the heart of God from all eternity—not as a device to meet an emergency, not as an instrument with which to extricate himself from some dilemma. We must preach the cross as a before-the-world-was highway —not as a postcreation bypath in the counsels of God. As the mind existed before the mental philosophy, as stars existed before Newton wrote his *Principia,* as this continent lay beyond the setting sun long before Columbus discovered it, as electricity was in the universe long before Edison; so the cross, not an episode but an eternal mood in God's heart, not an incident of Christ's life, not an accident in His career, not just a moral spectacle to exhibit God's love, but a transaction founded in deep necessity, was in heaven before it was on Calvary.

But Christ's face was set toward Calvary before aught of creation from the womb of nothingness came. And the centuries from Adam to Christ were crimson with the blood of innocent victims killed as types of the slain Lamb of God.

The diversified, systematic sacrifices of the Jews, like finger posts along the highway of time, pointed worshipers to a sacrificial Saviour. Significant shadows of redemptive entity still ahead, adumbrations of a substance yet to come, by the blood of a thousand altars, these sacrifices—elemental, preparatory, preliminary, rudimental, introductory—pointed to Christ, the propellent center to which the faith of mankind before and since gravitated.

Harry Rimmer wrote: "The cross on which the Saviour hung was not a tragic incident in the earth-life of the Son of God, but was rather the climax of a deliberate plan made in the councils of heaven—before the creation of the present order of the cosmos."

Before time commenced its solemn march did divine love consider man's ruined condition and resolved not to spare the greatest gift which either time could know or eternity produce. God's great love stretched out over the long centuries of time, but through the areas of eternity—a love that anticipated the vast need before it had arisen.

Thus in the cross, the supreme interpretation of God, we see that the agony of God over human sin is eternal—a focus in time and space of that travail which God bore, and bears, from the foundation of the world.

Him, being delivered by the determinate counsel and foreknowledge of God . . . crucified and slain (Acts 2:23).

. . . eternal life . . . promised before the world began (Titus 1:2).

. . . we speak the wisdom of God in a mystery . . . which God ordained before the world unto our glory (I Corinthians 2:7).

Knowing the end from the beginning (Isaiah 46:10):

His holy fingers formed the bough
Where grew the thorns that crowned His brow,

> The nails that pierced His hands were mined
> In secret places he designed.

Knowing that he was the Lamb slain from the foundation of the world (Revelation 13:8):

> He made the forests whence there sprung
> The tree on which His holy body hung,
> He died upon a cross of wood
> Yet made the hill upon which it stood.

Acquainted with the determinate counsel and foreknowledge of God:

> The sun which hid from Him its face
> By His decree was poised in space,
> The sky which darkened o'er His head
> By Him above the earth was spread.

Foreordained before the foundation of the world,

> The spear that spilt His precious blood
> Was tempered in the fires of God.
> The grave in which His form was laid
> Was hewn in rocks His hands had made.

We utterly despair of ever finding any words adequate to express so large a fact. Not for one minute was the cross an afterthought rill but a full and foreordained river coursing through God's ominiscient redemptive purpose.

Samuel Zwemer used to preach that the longest shadow in the world is the shadow of the cross. That luminous and glorious shadow reaches from the Upper Room where He entered, "the doors being shut," and showed them His hands and His side, bearing the scars of the piercing nails and savage Roman spear, to the empty tomb where Death, whose only flowers are faded garlands on coffin lids, could not wrap the Lily of the

Valley in icy and eternal cerements—when Death, whose only music is the sob of broken hearts, could not say to the mouth of Jesus, "Thou shalt never speak again"—where Death, whose only pleasure fountains are the falling tears of the world, could not say to the eyes of Jesus, "Thou shalt never see again."

And from that empty tomb that long cross-shadow reaches to Calvary's blood hill where the Prince of Life was slain by wicked hands and where, amid his agonies of body and soul, Midnight shoved Noonday, with her sun-bright garments, from the throne of the universe and sat himself upon the throne —spreading garments black as midnight's blackest blackness over all the earth. And from that bloodstained hill to the rough street where He fell beneath the weight of the cross and Simon was coerced into carrying the cross for the Calvary-bound Volunteer.

And from that street to Pilate's Judgment Hall—where, with lacerating scourge, they cut His naked back to shreds. And on to Gethsemane's garden, where the roots of His divine emotion put forth their crimson tears. And on to the Upper Room, where He changed wine into the perpetual symbol of His blood. And on to the Mount of Transfiguration where Moses and Elijah talked of His coming death (Matthew 17:3).

Reaching to the Jordan, where His burial in baptism foreshadowed His death.

Reaching to Nazareth where, by the toil of His hands and the sweat of His brow in the carpenter shop, He sanctified all labor.

Reaching to Bethlehem, "where that glorious form wherewith He wont at heaven's high council table to sit the midst of Tribal Unity He laid aside."

And from Bethlehem, where heaven put out its brightest

star to mark His birthplace, across four dumb centuries, and beyond, the cross throws its shadows and immortal radiance—to
Solomon's temple!

And over the victim, whether lamb, or bullock, or turtle dove,
on the altar of the Tabernacle. And over the bloodstained lintels
of the Passover night, where the keynote of the cross sounded
forth in the depths of remote antiquity and foreshadowed a
deliverance far greater.

And beyond that to the withered garden where Despair
pitched his pavilions upon the sterile and blasted fields of man's
lost estate. "And I will put enmity between thee and the woman,
and between thy seed and her seed; it shall bruise thy head, and
thou shalt bruise his heel" (Genesis 3:15).

That promise, dropped as a sun into man's sunless firmament,
was the center, prospectively, of all these constellations which
were to succeed each other in the darkness and illuminate that
long way unbroken from Eden to Calvary—Calvary, the abyss
of the world's greatest sorrow, the summit of the world's highest
hopes.

And our text is a sublime paraphrase of the Genesis verse,
substituting the language of fulfillment for the language of pre-
diction.

His death, prearranged, prophesied, provided by God (Genesis 22:8), was no afterthought. Jesus was born with the shadow
of the cross upon Him. With the shadow of the cross upon His
heart He learned to walk, He learned to talk, He learned to
work. From His earliest moment upon this earth it was His
burden by day, His pallet by night.

Shadow of the cross upon the Bethlehem swaddling clothes.

Shadow of the cross upon the road over which Joseph and

Mary, warned by an angel, and in fear of King Herod, fled to Egypt.

Shadow of the cross upon the waters of Lake Galilee—waters placid in the quiet of a peaceful day, or turbulent under the lash of a tempest.

Shadow of the cross on the well curb at Sychar, on the door of the temple, on sunrise, on sunset.

Shadow of the cross upon Gethsemane's garden.

The cross was with Him when they came with lanterns and torches to arrest the Light of the world.

The cross was with Him when Judas, one of the Twelve, betrayed him with a kiss which startled Him like the kiss of an adder and burned His cheek like hot coals.

The cross was with Him when Annas asked Him concerning His disciples and concerning His doctrine.

The cross was with Him when Caiaphas condemned Him.

The cross was with Him when Herod mocked Him.

He walked the streets dishonored by its shame. He climbed Olivet oppressed by its weight. He rose from the dead glorified by its sacrifice.

This gospel of the cross—simply, sublimely, and seriously stated—is our only watch cry of spiritual triumph in this day when everything for which apostles, martyrs, and reformers lived and died is being whittled away with disparagement that borders on devilishness—when there is hardly enough fire in men's hearts to melt the lead in their feet.

This message of the cross which our forefathers preached with rattle of chains amid the heat of the martyr's stake, in the darkness of dungeons and on torture racks, is *our* message, the message written in the blood of Christ and fastened with the nails of the cross. So we must—prayerfully, persistently, patiently—proclaim the cross. The cross, that which seemed to be Christ's shame, we must preach, glorying in what seemed to be the hour of His collapse, emphasizing what seemed to be His defeat.

If we do not do this our churches will be lighthouses without light, wells without water, dumb witnesses, sleeping watchman, silent trumpets, messengers without tidings, a comfort for infidels, jubilant joys to the devil, and an offense to God.

As to the preaching of the cross, there are some

IV. PERTINENT PARTICULARS OF PREACHING.

God's Word teaches that to the Jews who require a sign, the cross is a stumblingblock; and unto the Greeks, who seek after wisdom, foolishness (I Corinthians 1:22–23). Yet we are to preach the cross.

God's Word declares that to Jesus, the Author and Finisher of our faith, the cross was a shame (Hebrews 12:2). Yet we are to preach Christ crucified.

God's Word teaches that "the preaching of the cross is to them that perish foolishness, but unto us which are saved it is the power of God" (I Corinthians 1:18). We must preach the cross as the burden and symbol of Christ's suffering for sin. We read John 19:17–18. What else could such words mean?

We must preach the cross as the lowest rung in the ladder of Christ's obedience.

And being found in fashion as a man, he humbled himself, and became obedient unto death, even the death of the cross (Philippians 2:8).

We must preach the cross as the means by which reconciliation is made.

And, having made peace through the blood of his cross, by him to reconcile all things unto himself; by him, I say, whether they be things in earth, or things in heaven. And you, that were sometime alienated and enemies in your mind by wicked works, yet now hath he reconciled In the body of his flesh through death, to present you holy and unblameable and unreproveable in his sight (Colossians 1:20–22).

We must preach the cross as the remover of the curse of the law and the crucified Christ as the cancellation of the claims of the law.

For as many as are of the works of the law are under the curse: for it is written, Cursed is every one that continueth not in all things which are written in the book of the law to do them (Galatians 3:10).

But we also read:

Christ hath redeemed us from the curse of the law, being made a curse for us: for it is written, Cursed is every one that hangeth on a tree (Galatians 3:13).

God's word teaches that the law observances were abolished in Christ, for we read:

Blotting out the handwriting of ordinances that was against us, which was contrary to us, and took it out of the way, nailing it to his cross; And having spoiled principalities and powers, he made a shew of them openly, triumphing over them in it (Colossians 2:14–15).

Paul spoke of the cross as an offense (Galatians 5:11). He knew that the cross obtrudes like a barrier athwart the common track of man's common mind. He knew, even as we have been slow to learn, that the cross throws man's reckonings into confusion, and is significant of shame, failure, defeat, dishonor. The cross offends man's mental pride, confronting his speculative ingenuity as a piece of unmitigated absurdity.

The cross is an offense today to man's morality and the claims thereof because the cross shows that man's works cannot justify.

Knowing that a man is not justified by the works of the law, but by the faith of Jesus Christ, even we have believed in Jesus Christ, that we might be justified by the faith of Christ, and not by the works of the law: for by the works of the law shall no flesh be justified (Galatians 2:16).

The cross is an offense to philosophy—because the cross appeals to faith and not to reason, and rebukes and condemns the philosophies that substitute logic for the logic of events. The cross is an offense to man's will—because it calls for man's unconditional surrender.

The cross, where Jesus expended the crimson cash of His precious blood, is an offense for wealth—because it shows how Jesus who was rich for our sakes became poor and because it demands that we love God with our pocketbooks as well as with our hearts.

The cross is an offense to pride—because it declares how Jesus "humbled himself, and became obedient unto death, even the death of the cross" (Philippians 2:8).

The cross is an offense to sin—because the cross, through Him who "bore our sins in his own body on the tree," shows God's estimate and God's hatred of sin.

The cross is an offense to the devil—because it is written: "And they overcame him [the devil] by the blood of the Lamb . . ." (Revelation 12:11).

The cross is an offense to all bloodless cults and preaching—

because it shows that "without the shedding of blood there is no remission of sins."

The cross is an offense to men's hatreds—because it is the most superlative example of Love the world knows, can know, will know.

The cross is an offense to the universalists—because it declares that everybody is not saved, not brought from death unto life. Only one of the two thieves was saved, and he by faith.

The cross is an offense to infidelity—because it enthrones faith over reason, God's commandments above maxims of men, God's declaratives of creation over and above the doctrine of chance.

The cross must be the central theme of our preaching, the highway along which we march with steady feet, not a bypath we stroll timidly and carelessly along.

The cross must be the centrality of our preaching as long as sin kindles a blush of shame, as long as there are eyes to glisten with tears of pentinence, as long as erring mortals need to close the door on bad yesterdays, as long as the music of consolation is needed where sorrow reigns, as long as Death drops a curtain around an evening sleeper, as long as the Angel of Hope hangs her lamp from the lintel and waits for the morning, as long as in this world there are the works of the flesh which are "adultery, fornication, uncleanness, lasciviousness, idolatry, witchcraft, hatred, variance, emulations, wrath, strife, seditions, heresies, envyings, murders, drunkenness, revellings," and such like. Just as long will the cross be the center of all God-guided battles that end in victory. As long as there is in the churches the need for the fruit of the Spirit—love, joy, peace, long-suffering, gentleness, goodness, meekness, faith, self-control—

just so long will the cross be the center of all God-pleasing life.

Preaching the cross, we will in particular preach:

A. *The terror of sin.*

Wherefore, as by one man sin entered into the world, and death by sin; and so death passed upon all men, for that all have sinned. . . . And not as it was by one that sinned, so is the gift: for the judgment was by one to condemnation, but the free gift is of many offences unto justification. . . . Therefore as by the offence of one judgment came upon all men to condemnation; even so by the righteousness of one the free gift came upon all men unto justification of life. For as by one man's disobedience many were made sinners, so by the obedience of one shall many be made righteous" (Romans 5:12, 16, 18, 19).

So the cross testifies to the most terrible fact in God's universe—the ghastly, gruesome, ghoulish fact of sin.

Sin, a breach in the moral order and harmony of the universe, works confusing disintegration and certain death.

Sin, a conspiracy against the sovereignty of God, is a contradiction of God's nature, an insult to His holiness. There is no term expressive of reproach, expressive of shame, expressive of misery that the cross does not set forth to portray the terror of sin, just as there is no image that can produce aversion or fear that is not employed by the Scriptures to represent sin.

Sin is what made the cross a necessity.

Sin—Life's most dreadful and inexorable curse.

Sin—the desert breath that drinks up every dew.

Sin—the death-head set amidst Life's feast.

Sin—the power that reversed man's nature, destroyed the harmony of his powers, threw him woefully deranged, miserable, ungoverned, lost—into interminable leagues of night.

Sin—the evil that subverted the constitutional order of man's nature, dismantled man of his nobility, brought man in unconditional surrender to diabolical power, caused man treacherously to give up the keys of the soul-citadel placed in his keeping.

Sin—a fatal mischief of the heart, a seed big with future pain and grief, a hot sirocco blasting all gardens, the quintessence of all horrors, the causative element of all world suffering, a perpetual lava rush scorching all green fields.

Sin—a madness in the brain, a poison in the heart, an opiate in the will, a frenzy in the imagination, a black darkness that invests man's whole moral being, the intolerable burden of a soul destined to live forever. The one word with which we can write all world tragedies.

Sin! The flowers of it grow among skulls and have no perfume.

Sin! The crowns of it are made of thorns sharper than bayonet points and are heavier than iron jackets.

Sin! The dances of it are the dances of death.

Sin! The gardens of it are full of Satan's poison ivy—gardens loathesome and desolate.

Sin! The wages of it is death.

Sin! The honey of it is gall.

Sin! The freedom of it is bitter bondage.

Sin! The health of it is disease.

Sin! The music of it is ear-killing discord.

Sin! The revelry of it is burlesque.

Sin! The splendors of it are faded spangles.

Sin! The pleasures of it are ghastly pictures.

Sin! The voyage of it is perilous with rocks and treacherous shoals.

Sin! The clothing of it is the poisonous shirt of Nessus.

Sin! The day of it is horrible night.

The eternal issue of sin is called into question at Christ's cross —because God's justice demands retribution for sin unless sin be atoned for. Preaching the crucified Christ, we declare that at the cross every righteous judgment of God is perfectly met —because the righteousness of God cannot exist if sin is condoned.

Christ crucified is the terrible consummate testimony of what sin is. We trace sin's power everywhere, we see and feel sin's woe. But we come to the profoundest knowledge of and the profoundest hatred of sin when we see that it crucified Christ.

All this means that in our thinking of the cross and in our preaching of the cross, we must, in particular, abhor:

B. *Light conceptions of sin.*

Seeing sin through the crimson lenses of Calvary's cross, there will be no holding or setting forth sin as a disagreeable hindrance to the smooth on-going of the social machinery, sin as an upward stumble in man's progress, sin as psychic rebellion or egotistic abnormality, sin as nightmare caused by too much appetite and too little digestion; sin just perverted taste, sin just and only goodness in the making, sin just and only the backward pull of outworn good; sin just and only an illusion of the mortal mind, sin just and only as a rash, sin just and only a penknife for dainty manicuring, never a guillotine with the power of decapitation.

At the cross these terrible identities of sin come out. All that we have ever done to make this earth a different place from the holy ground on which the holy God might have walked in perfect oneness with obedient children; all our wilfulness, disobedience, untruth, passion, lust, jealousy, selfishness, wickedness, yea, *all* take their place *in* and declare their oneness *with* sin that brought Christ to Calvary's cross. Looking toward the cross, let us not forget that we killed Him—you and I.

Look upon Him whom we pierced. Our sins were the evil tongues that maligned Christ. Our sins were the dirty mouths that befouled His face with dirty sputum. Our sins were the hard palms that slapped Him. Our sins were the knuckled fists that pummelled His face. Our sins were the scourges that cut His back to shreds. Our sins were the thorns that punctured His brow. Our sins were used to build the cross on which He died. Our sins were the nails that pierced His sacred hands and tore through the tendons of His feet. Our sins were the hammers that drove the nails. Our sins were the wagging heads that mocked Him when, hanging on the cross, His every breath was a pang of pain, His every heartbeat a throb of agony.

Our sins made Him become all that God must judge. Our sins made His sinless soul an offering.

> My sins laid open to the rod
> The back which from the law was free,
> And the eternal Son of God
> Received the stripes once due to me.
> The sponge of vinegar and gall
> By me was placed upon His tongue,
> And when derision mocked His call,
> *I* stood the mocking crowd among.

Christ's crucifixion, the work of the whole race, must shock until we hate what caused Him all the agonies of body and torture of soul on the cross, until we look with horror upon our hands red with His blood, until every heart must mourn His death of fearsome horrors as its own bloody, butcherous, wicked, murderous deed.

Just as we see Nicodemus in all his judicial pride was there when they crucified Jesus, so we with respect to academic respect, with pride of social standing, were there when they crucified our Lord.

Just as Judas Iscariot, with covetous greed that caused him to cry out against the woman who anointed Jesus and caused him to sell Jesus for thirty pieces of silver and betray the Master with a kiss, was there when they crucified the Christ—so we, with covetous greed that makes us stingy and rob God in our giving, were there.

Just as the envious and selfish Pharisees were there, so we, if we are victims of selfishness, were there when they crucified Christ. And selfishness is the abnormality of life, the apostasy of being, the suicide of greatness, the downfall of the soul. Just as selfishness dug the first grave that ever marred the face of the earth, made Jacob a cheat and Absalom a rebel, made a thief of Judas, made liars of Annanias and Sapphira, so also selfishness made us to have part in the crucifixion of Christ.

Just as Peter, the coward, though not in sight when they crucified the Lord, was represented by Fear at the cross, so we, guilty oft of spiritual cowardice in churches and communities, were there when they crucified our Lord.

Herod Antipas, powerfully ruling one-fourth part of the Roman Empire, with no regard for the moral and spiritual decencies of life, caring only for the satisfaction of his personal lust, the rattlesnake before whom Jesus was tried—this filthy scoundrel who sent Jesus away to be crucified was there. So we, slaves of sensuality deeply embedded in the heart of modern life were there when they crucified our Lord.

And some who saw all the crucifixion horrors, some from near and some from afar, were indifferent and blind to the significance of it all; so we, if we find ourselves guilty of indifference, were there when they crucified our Lord.

Yes, we were there. The mob was there. Herod and Herodias were there. Peter was there. Judas Iscariot was there. Nicodemus was there. Governor Pilate was there. The rich Joseph of Arimathea was there. In fact the whole human race was there. We all had part in it. "All we like sheep have gone astray." "All have sinned." And as we all gathered at the cross to crucify the Lord with our sin, so we must gather at the cross to be delivered from our sin, which is to say Christ's irreproachable life, Christ's matchless teaching, Christ's astonishing miracles, Christ's marvelous example would have availed nothing for our salvation had they not found consummation in Calvary's cross.

Incidental and collateral all these to the one purpose for which He came: to die, that man born once and born dead might be born again and born alive.

Not by His sinless life was Jesus man's substitute.

Not by His miracles did He honor the law, satisfy justice, meet the demands of divine holiness.

Not by His teachings did He take away humanity's despairing woe and God's judgment upon the human race.

Not by His beautiful example did He take our place under the law.

Not by His preaching did He open a fountain for all uncleanness.

Not by His character did He repair the insulted dignity of

God's nature by a reparation equal in merits to the character of the insulted dignity itself.

Only by suffering the death which was expiatory with reference to God, which was punishment with reference to men, did He adequately compensate God's government by an equivalent for man's offense—offer a boundless mercy in terms consistent with the integrity of the moral law.

The great salient is that Jesus Christ died. Jesus Christ died an *initial* death—as the Lamb of God slain from the foundation of the world. Jesus Christ died an *official* death—as the God-selected substitute. Jesus Christ died a *judicial* death—the judgment death for others. Jesus Christ died a *sacrificial* death —the Just for the unjust, that He might bring us to God. And in dying so, Jesus Christ retrod the way of man's retreat, liquidated the bond of inexorable Law, sheathed the sword of Justice behind the blood-drenched Mercy Seat. Then God's perfections opened wide their arms repentant sinners to receive.

And what is humanity profited if we shine with haloes of academic luster, if we preach not the cross where the history of human guilt culminates?

What are souls profited if we speak with the tongues of men and of angels and preach not the cross where the purposes of divine love are made intelligible?

Where are we and lost souls profited if we shine with the luster of theological splendor, if we preach not the truth that the rays of glory emanating from Christ are focused in the cross?

What wisdom show we when we use educational fingers to point men from blind alleys of ignorance to highways of knowledge if we preach not that the fingers of prophecy point to the cross, the true center and sanctuary of this fallen and broken world?

What sense show we if we try to describe the meaning of Daniel's image, "with his head of fine gold, with his breast and arms of silver, and his belly and thighs of brass, with his eyes of iron, with his feet part of iron and part of clay," if we preach not that the hieroglyphics of the Old Testament types find their key at the cross?

What are we and others profited when we show wisdom enough to solve many domestic and political problems if we preach not that the greatest problem of all, the problem of human redemption, is solved only at the cross?

What are we and others profited when we open doors into the areas of mysteries if we preach not that the door of heaven is opened at the cross, if we do not declare that the cross is the key given of God to unlock the vaults of great treasures in all spheres?

Of what value is our knowledge of Hebrew and our cleverness in Greek if we preach not Christ's cross where the serpent's head is bruised?

What is it worth to the world for all our colleges and seminaries to be accredited by the highest requirements of accreditation if they send not our preachers and missionaries to preach the Christ's cross where the bitters of life are sweetened, where earthly glory fades, where the world is stripped of its charms?

What is our preparation for preaching worth to us and to the unsaved millions of earth if we preach not the cross where the penal claims of God against sinners are exhausted? If we preach not the cross where the fires of the law are extinguished?

What are we worth to the Christ of the cross if we preach

with the eloquence of Demosthenes and preach not the cross where the righteous judgment of God is met?

Do we deserve any praise if, with summa cum laude on diplomas and with honorary degrees, we preach not the cross where the sinner's condemnation is lifted and the sinner's death sentence revoked?

What reward deserve we if we give our bodies to be burned and bestow all our goods to feed the poor, if we preach not the cross where every righteous judgment of God is met through the perfectly righteous Christ who was judged as an unrighteous One that we, the unrighteous ones, might be judged as righteous?

How can we other than miserable comforters be to those in grief if we preach not the cross where all human sorrows hide in His wounds?

How can we claim not to be truant and traitorous to Truth if we preach not the cross where the shadows of Death are dispelled, where the darkness of Eternity is irradiated?

How can we claim to be doctrinally sound if we preach not that the great events of the gospel yield their importance to Christ's cross, even as the great doctrines of Grace revolve around the cross?

Can we claim to be other than sinfully ignorant if we know not and declare not that Christ's incarnation was preparatory to the cross, that the Transfiguration foreshadowed the cross, that the Resurrection was the complement of the cross and Pentecost the fruit of the cross?

Can we claim we contend for the faith once for all delivered if we preach not Christ's cross of atonement where every sin is met and conquered, every darkness met and dispelled, every iniquity confronted and killed, every question faced and an-

swered, every foe fought and defeated, every fear met and
quenched, every hunger satisfied, every sorrow assuaged?

How can we claim to be God's ambassadors if we go not
forth to preach the cross as the true center and sanctuary of
this sin-cursed, head-dizzy, war-burdened, satellite-startled
world—the only leverage mighty enough to roll off crushed
humanity the ponderous incubus which bondage to Satan has
placed upon it?

Let us make Christ's cross an experience in our own lives.
Make the mercies and love of God make us to put into deeds the
words and truths of the hymn:

> When I survey the wondrous cross,
> On which the Prince of glory died,
> My richest gain I count but loss,
> And pour contempt on all my pride.
>
> Forbid it, Lord, that I should boast,
> Save in the death of Christ, my God;
> All the vain things that charm me most,
> I sacrifice them to His blood.
>
> See, from His head, His hands, His feet,
> Sorrow and love flow mingled down;
> Did e'er such love and sorrow meet,
> Or thorns compose so rich a crown?
>
> Were the whole realm of nature mine,
> That were a present far too small;
> Love so amazing, so divine,
> Demands my soul, my life, my all.

And may we practice this hymn until Jesus shall come again
or until the holy and beloved hands pierced on Calvary's cross
that opened to us the gates to Grace shall open to us the gates
to Glory—beyond which we shall walk and talk with the Christ

who was on the cross the *submissive* Lamb of God (Isaiah 53: 1–5), the *substitutionary* Lamb of God (Isaiah 53:6–15), the *suffering* Lamb of God (Matthew 27:27–34), the *sacrificial* Lamb of God (Matthew 27:35–56), the *silent* Lamb of God (Matthew 27:57–60 and Isaiah 53:42–47)—concerning whom we read:

The four and twenty elders fall down before him that sat on the throne, and worship him that liveth for ever and ever, and cast their crowns before the throne, saying, Thou art worthy, O Lord, to receive glory and honour and power . . . (Revelation 4:10–11).

And concerning whom we read again:

And I beheld, and I heard the voice of many angels round about the throne and the beasts and the elders: and the number of them was ten thousand times ten thousand, and thousands of thousands; Saying with a loud voice, Worthy is the Lamb that was slain to receive power, and riches, and wisdom, and strength, and honour, and glory, and blessing (Revelation 5:11–12).

2 Linked Lives

For none of us liveth to himself, and no man dieth to himself (Romans 14:7).

I think of:

I. A GREAT PREACHER'S PEN.

The Apostle Paul, a preacher who compassed the earth with the truths of redemption and left a trail of gospel glory across the Gentile world, counted all things but loss that he might know Jesus and the power of His resurrection and the fellowship of Christ's suffering. Taking pleasure in infirmities, reproaches, necessities, persecutions and distresses for Christ's sake (II Corinthians 12:10), he found his heavenly call to be the spiritual melody of his earthly walk. Reaching and rescuing some in preaching by word of mouth, he has reached millions with his pen from which gospel truths dropped like golden pollen from the stems of shaken lilies.

One truth from his pen I would have you pitch your mental tents upon in this notable hour—and always: "For none of us liveth to himself, and no man dieth to himself" (Romans 14:7).

That statement, one of Paul's profound sociological and spiritual assertions, declares that we live linked lives.

The matter of linked lives makes us to think upon:

II. OUR EPOCH.

The course of human progress is marked by epochs. Modern history records four epochs: Feudalism, Renaissance, Reformation, Revolution. Each of these epochs had a distinctive character; and each made a distinctive contribution to man's material and spiritual life. The Feudal Age was distinctly military, the Renaissance definitely intellectual, the Reformation vividly religious, the Revolution positively political.

The Feudal Age gave kings and constitutions on the material side, and on the spiritual side deep respect for order and authority.

The Renaissance gave a rich literature, broad vision, and freedom of thought.

The Reformation gave a broader tolerance in the human mind.

The Revolution gave a republican form of government and wrought in man the self-reliance of democracy. The epochs made their contribution and are passed away. Yet these epochs were linked eras.

The epoch in which we live is as different in character from the four epochs mentioned as they are different from one another. Yet in our era we live linked lives—lives linked not to one unit but to many, and reaching out in every direction.

Today, as we consider lofty concerns of the soul, the epoch in which our lives are inevitably linked with others is accused of "clowning on a time-bomb," of "running on the moral momentum of a godly ancestry," of calling man "an animated event in time and space and the fortuitous concourse of points of energy," of giving refuge to some who would (if they could) make this "land of the free and the home of the brave" the land of the spree and the home of the rave.

Today there is the tendency to idolize science so that many undertake to interpret all things in terms of natural phenomena which reduces the supernatural to ignorance. Tragic is the reduction of Christianity to the status of humanism, social service, and national or individual therapy, with the resulting tendency to undermine faith.

In America, *now,* are the evils that caused multi-palaced Babylon to become an animal-prowling jungle; evils that made Rome, with her close-meshed code of laws and victorious legions, to collapse from the inside; evils that made glorious Greece of old to become only a crust in history's garbage can; evils that changed wealthy, Nile-fertilized Egypt into a shabby sexton of tombs; evils that made ancient Spain, with her piratical ships that harassed all seas and filled her coffers with gold, to become a drowsy beggar watching a broken clock; evils that made mighty Nineveh to become a dirty doormat for wicked feet; evils that made Tyre of old a skeletonized horror.

Today many give ear to advocacies that terminate in a whirlpool and never inspire men to nobility of life, never give men wisdom and courage to scorn the soft pillows of luxury and "endure hardness as a good soldier of Jesus Christ" (II Timothy 2:3).

The youth of this country has not experienced the weight of years and the departure of unrecoverable strength. The capital of their youth has not been wasted in unprofitable investments. Their feet are not leaden. Their spirits "challenge the blithe audacity of Shelley's lark." Yet their eyes have seen on TV the mushroom cloud of the horrible hydrogen device unleashing explosive violence so tremendous that it thunderously and terrifyingly prophesies a weapon that would possess the concentrated force of twenty million tons of TNT—weighing ten times that of all the bombs dropped by all American airplanes in the last world war.

Their world is mounted on a wild Pegasus they cannot control. Darkness deepens. Terrifying vistas of destruction and death open on world horizons. As in Noah's day "the earth is corrupt before God, and filled with violence." The onward march of Russia is a stupefying phenomenon that has no parallel in history—and, in the last few years, six hundred million people have come under Russia's slave rule. World situations point to a strife of such fearful proportions that the survival of the human race is a matter of immediate concern. The world is hanging on a thread above an abyss—"quivering on the brink of a catastrophe that will end the world." The secular dream of history as an evolution into perfection is the most gigantic delusion in the history of human thought. The neurotic school of fiction is a give-away to the insecurity of the modern mind. The sexual novel furnishes a symptom of the same fumbling grasp of reality. Dr. Gordon Clark, a leading Christian professor of philosophy, says: "From all that can be seen now, humanism and communistic hatred of Christianity will be the prevalent philosophy of the coming age."

While we protest the progressive surrender of public schools to forces of irreligion, a Columbia University professor calls the Christian religion "a compensatory fiction for an inner feeling of inferiority, an importation of symbols into a world of fact." Perhaps T. S. Eliot had such insanity in mind when he wrote:

In the land of lobelias and tennis flannels
The rabbit shall burrow and the thorn revisit,
The nettle shall flower on the gravel court,
And the wind shall say, "Here were decent godless people:
Their only monument the asphalt road
And a thousand lost golf balls. . . ."

The world is one of divisive and appallingly subversive forces, exultantly operative, where nations seem to be in the grip of a planetary nightmare. And I am no photographer of sordid spots in saying so.

Now think of our linkage to:

III. THE PAST—AS BENEFICIARIES.

Edmund Burke said: "Civilization is a contract between the great dead, the living, and the unborn." Thus he shows our un-cancellable contracts with the past, the present, the future—to which we are linked like Alpine mountain climbers.

Linked to the past, debtors we are to the great dead. Rich our social and spiritual capital—rich in treasures from the past. Priceless trophies have we from battles never to be fought again. Examining our capital, we see that the social orchards that furnish fruit for us and the spiritual trees that shelter us have rootage in ancient graves.

In all our capital we see the consecrated blood of yesterday. Ringing church bells echo with the groans of all who died in struggles for religious freedom. The Bible, supernatural Book—so unlike all books in height, depth, breadth, universality, sweep, and glory—is stained with the tears and blood of those who stood for it on torture rack, in jail, in exile. But for them we would not have the Book through which God speaks, tells us

His will, utters His commands, makes His appeals, gives His promises, tells His love, reveals His character.

Much medicine used for lessening human anguish is mixed with the blood of martyrs who suffered and died that the world might win its battle against disease. The heaven-descending mercies of anaesthesia cause us to acknowledge our debt to those who became targets of sneer, jeer, and vilification to rob operations of terror and pain. Much we enjoy of civil, intellectual, and religious hope is but the moral courage, intellectual perception, and spiritual suffering of the past appearing in new and resplendent forms. Man is like the limb. He has relations to the tree that bore him, and indeed is linked to all creation. This linkage is of dependence and obligation. To his ancestry man is indebted for his physical basis and mental bias. To society man is indebted for security of person and property. To the world of yesterday he is indebted for ideas and discoveries that make up his mental furniture—to the world today for many of his highest incentives and inspirations. Man is also a retainer and pensioner upon the bounties of nature. Forests, planets, fields, seas, mines, mountains, furnish his stuff to work on. Well may every man echo the words of Childe Harold:

> I live not in myself, but I become
> Portion of that around me.

This linkage of dependence, whether upon man or nature, carries with it the relation of obligation. Freely man has received; freely man is to give.

Virgil said that when Aeneas tore the bough from the myrtle tree, it exuded blood. That tree, giving forth blood, is a symbol of our forefathers who, through movements of retrogressive tendency, through pestilence and flame and flood, translated the principles of liberty and equality into permanent institutions. We drink from wells we did not dig, reap from fields we did not sow, enjoy glories and privileges for which we toiled not nor spun, and obtained without hardships or sufferings.

We are Saxons—debtors to Hampden and Cromwell.

We are Puritans—debtors to Vane and Robinson.

We are Southerners—debtors to Calhoun and Lee.

We are Northerners—debtors to Beecher and Longfellow.

We are Americans—debtors to Washington, Webster, Lincoln, and others who counted not their lives dear unto themselves.

Not only so. We are linked to:

IV. THE PRESENT—AS BENEFACTORS.

Our linkage to the living is momentous in opportunities and responsibilities.

In other years Julius Caesar laid the foundation stones of a great empire. Socrates aroused the young men of Athens. Savonarola, under God, revived the city of Florence. Columbus discovered a new world. Luther had part in rebuking a corrupt church. Wycliffe kindled fires of reformation. Washington established democracy in a new hemisphere. Lincoln signed the emancipation proclamation for four million slaves. Joan of Arc led the armies of France to victory. Cromwell stretched a psalm into a war drum and dissolved a parliament. Beethoven "made surging seas of tone subservient to his rod" as he touched the world's harp strings. Angelo "raised children unto God from the sterile womb of stone." Florence Nightingale bandaged the world's battle wounds. Dorothea Dix soothed the crazed brain. John Howard poured fresh air into the lazaretto. David Brainerd changed savage warwhoops into Sabbath songs. David Livingstone opened in Africa the highway, marked now by the tomb-stones of martyr missionaries, over which Ethiopia stumbles with outstretched hands toward God. Gutenberg, with his moveable type printing press, opened blind alleys of ignorance into endless highways of wisdom.

Our debt to them and their example urges us in our today to be courageous and take care of liberty, to be wise and take care of justice, to be Christianly patriotic and help America weigh worthily on God's scales, to measure tall by God's measuring rod—speaking and living so that all duty shall be transformed into spiritual power. With gratitude to great men who have gone before, with determination to perpetuate the priceless principles of political and economic freedom that were born of the brain and bought with the blood of the founding fathers, we must live unselfishly with and for those with whom our lives are everywhere linked.

We must die to some things before we can greatly live for others—even as Carey died to leather that he might live to missions, as Wilberforce died to fashion to live to simplicity, as Ruskin died to gold to live to beauty, as Brooks died to law to live unto the gospel, as Grenfell died to comfort to live to medical ministry in bleak Labrador. Thus we can produce soul fruit.

The first business of a nation is the production of souls of good quality. Only as a nation bears soul fruit is she great by the definitions of greatness found in God's dictionary. Bearing soul fruit, America is worth living for and worth dying for—as our nation answers the call to supreme self-surrender to God—and for God, for America, for the world.

I believe that this nation has been a thought in the mind of God from all eternity for this very hour. Believing that, we must believe that if the spiritual fails, the success of the material is worth little at the last.

What are we profited if, citizens of a civilization that makes ice in the tropics, we attack no frigid conventionalities with holy, spiritual impetuosity? Or, if using telescopes to see worlds millions of miles away, we get in fog banks and lose sight of God? Or, if adding radios to our ears, we have deaf ears to the voice of God? Or, if listening to great choirs, we miss life's central melody and become victims of dawdling ditties? Or, if adding telephones to our tongues, we have little of spiritual worth to say? Or, if building skyscrapers, we teach not that "other foundation can no man lay than that is laid, which is Jesus Christ" (I Corinthians 3:11). Or, if writing around the world with the telegraph, we fail to write the literature of godliness upon the fleshly tablets of human hearts? Or, if flying swifter and mounting higher than eagles with our airplanes, we are slow in service—and follow Christ limpingly and complainingly?

Today calls for heroism—as we reckon with the perversities and departures of the present time. What is heroism? Not being shrunken and decrepit, giving only an insignificant shadow of Christianity, showing a tame-heartedness.

Dr. Coward, once speaking of such tiptoeing timidity, said: "The eagle of the height has been tamed into a little bird that eats out of your hand, glad of getting a crumb. We have more or less exchanged Niagara, with its tremendous sweep, for the sluggish canal with its slow movement. We have more or less exchanged the tide for the ripple of the pond. We have forgotten the splendor of the sunshine, in the satisfaction which we feel in the candlelight."

That is not heroism. The heroism needed is the heroism which, with undying purpose, red-hot convictions, with firmness in hours of peril, dares speak and live the truth that when Christianity goes, civilization goes. And if Christianity goes, there is nothing to live for. Byron, in his poem "Darkness," gives us the picture of just what would happen:

> . . . The world was void,
> The populous and the powerful was a lump,
> Seasonless, herbless, treeless, manless, lifeless—
> A lump of death—a chaos of hard clay.
> The rivers, lakes, and ocean all stood still,
> And nothing stirr'd within their silent depths;
> Ships sailorless lay rotting on the sea,
> And their masts fell down piecemeal; as they dropp'd,
> They slept on the abyss without a surge—
> The waves were dead; the tides were in their grave,
> The moon, their mistress, had expired before;
> The winds were wither'd in the stagnant air,
> And the clouds perish'd; Darkness had no need
> Of aid from them—She was the universe.

Darkness like doom will settle upon the modern and spiritual world if the religion of Jesus should be taken away.

In gratitude to the great dead, in acknowledgment of all duties to the living, we remember that our lives are linked to:

V. POSTERITY—AS BEQUEATHERS.

The past is gone forever into the tomb of Time. The present is passing, and we cannot hold it. Worthily must we pay our debt to the dead, meet the demands of the living, and hand down to posterity our blood-bequeathed legacies unreduced in quality and in quantity.

Because of the immortality of influence, men are linked to all tomorrows. Creatures of a day, men do not close their account with the world at their death. Much about men cannot be put in a coffin and buried in a cemetery. Statesmen of wicked laws live in those laws, cursing successive generations. Authors of base books survive in those books like a chronic pestilence. Libertines who set corrupting fashions live in these fashions as a plague. Long after men die, they agitate currents of world thought and life. When nobody remembers the house in which we live, our image will remain among men, in evil or righteousness, influencing posterity.

We must not pose before posterity nor attitudinize before the unborn years. As we are beneficiaries so must we be benefactors, making social and spiritual bequeathments to those who come after. The men who sought to establish in America a government of the free were blessed by God, whose worship they came to maintain, whose truth they were to transmit to posterity. If we fail to live as they lived and dedicate not ourselves to the preservation of our heritage, justice will forsake the laws they gave, liberty will flee our institutions, and glory will depart from our nation.

May our youth call it wisdom to bleed to bless, to lose their lives to find them, to unyoke tyrannies of the flesh, to be hinges on great gates God shall swing open, to take from their thrones evils coiled thereon like adders. They must be bequeathers whose ancestral glory shall be a lamp unto the feet and a light to the path to posterity. Thus shall they illustrate the truth that "Abel being dead yet speaketh"—and, as it was with Lincoln, so shall they be found in life and after death, anywhere except in the tomb.

> And so they buried Lincoln? Strange and vain
> Has any creature thought of Lincoln hid

In any vault 'neath any coffin lid,
In all the years since that wild spring of pain?
'Tis false—he never in the grave hath lain.
You could not bury him although you slid
Upon his clay the Cheops pyramid
Or heaped it with Rocky Mountain chain.
They slew themselves—they but set Lincoln free;
And in all the earth his great heart beats as strong,
Shall beat while pulses throb to chivalry;
And burn with hate of tyranny and wrong.
Whoever will may find him anywhere
Save in the tomb—not there!—he is not there.

Standing now on an ever-moving present between an irretrievable past and a challenging future, I would have you reach a colossal conclusion, which is that you must be linked to the

VI. PERSON OR PERSONS—AS BELIEVERS.

That Person of persons is King of kings and Lord of lords—to whom God hath given a name above every name, Jesus Christ, Son of man without sin and Son of God with power! Jesus said: "I am the vine, ye are the branches . . . without me ye can do nothing" (John 15:5). Having union with Jesus, as vine with branch, we shall be fruitful unto good works, meeting wisely the Christian obligation of personal righteousness found only in Christ. He only is Literature's loftiest ideal, Philosophy's highest personality, Criticism's supreme problem, Theology's fundamental doctrine—and personally, socially, politically, religiously, educationally, scientifically, nationally, internationally, the only hope of our head-dizzy, body-weary, soul-sick, war-wounded, sin-smitten world.

"Without me ye can do nothing." The branch has nothing

but what it gets in linkage with the vine—and you and I can have nothing but what we get from Jesus. His life, truth, and blood—as so many articulate words—plead for law, freedom, fidelity, eternity, and life for all men.

"In him was life; and the life was the light of men" (John 1:4).

Jesus said: "I am come a light into the world, that whosoever believeth on me should not abide in darkness" (John 12:46).

". . . I am the light of the world: he that followeth me shall not walk in darkness, but shall have the light of life" (John 8:12).

"As long as I am in the world, I am the light of the world" (John 9:5).

". . . he that walketh in darkness knoweth not whither he goeth" (John 12:35).

But Paul says: ". . . Christ shall give thee light" (Ephesians 5:14).

Only when Christ becomes the light of men can there be anything but dense darkness—individual darkness, home darkness, school darkness, community darkness, city darkness, national darkness, world darkness. Without Christ, the Life and Light of men, every light man has will flicker and fail as candles placed in a tunnel through which fierce winds blow.

All great reformations that have been to the world as plenteous rain upon drought-smitten fields, all changes that have been to mankind as bread in time of famine, and all exchanges of light for darkness have been due to the fact that God's life—Christ—became the light of men.

Christ, whose life is the light of men, offers himself to you—to manifest his life in your body (II Corinthians 4:10), to think through your mind, to love through your heart, to speak through your mouth, to look through your eyes, to hear through your ears, to work through your hands, to walk through your feet in paths of righteousness that grow brighter and brighter unto the perfect day.

Christ is the power and wisdom of God in the entirety of man's life. Paul says: ". . . Christ in you the hope of glory" (Colossians 1:27). That glory is the glory of Christly character here and now, of deliverance from the smiling ease with which faith in eternal things is thrown off and doubts and lesser truths grinningly taken on, of freedom from intellectual conceit unaware of the rattle of its dry bones, yes, the glory of deliverance from contracting spiritual boundaries while extending intellectual frontiers, of deliverance from superficial mental illumination that lacks the urge of sacrificial passion—the glory of Christ enunciating Himself within the precincts of your personality.

To keep Christ off the throne of your life is like taking heat out of fire, melody out of music, color out of rainbows, numbers out of mathematics, water out of the ocean, mind out of metaphysics, sap out of trees, all light out of day—because:

> Christ is the power of God to guide you,
> Christ is the might of God to uphold you,
> Christ is the wisdom of God to teach you,
> Christ is the eye of God to watch over you,
> Christ is the ear of God to hear you,
> Christ is the Word of God to give you speech,
> Christ is the hand of God to protect you,
> Christ is the shield of God to shelter you,
> Christ is the host of God to defend you.

Yielding yourself completely to Him, you will be capable of great usefulness and development. If you had at the outset the capacity of a teaspoon, you may, by doing His will, have the capacity of an ocean bed—the capacity to lose the less to find the greater, to lose the outward to find the inward, to lose semblance to find realities. Therefore, I urge you to say in prayer:

To be united, Lord, with Thee,
As branch with tree,
   For this I pray.

To draw my power, Lord, from Thee,
As branch from tree,
   For this I pray.

To bear my fruit, O Lord, from Thee (be wholly Thine),
As branch from tree,
   For this I pray.

3 The *Must* of the Second Birth

Jesus answered and said unto him, Verily, verily, I say unto thee, Except a man be born again, he cannot see the kingdom of God. . . . That which is born of the flesh is flesh; and that which is born of the Spirit is spirit. Marvel not that I said unto thee, Ye must be born again (John 3:3, 6–7).

The whole Bible is important. "All scripture . . . is profitable . . ." (II Timothy 3:16). Every great Christian doctrine is explained somewhere in the Bible.

Hebrews 11 deals with the subject of *faith*.

I Corinthians 13 deals with the subject of *love*.

I Corinthians 15 deals with the subject of the *resurrection*.

The first part of John 3 deals with *regeneration*—setting forth the nature and necessity of being born again. The important truth is not set before us by means of profound theological statements, but by means of a nighttime conversation which took place between Jesus and a man named Nicodemus.

Milton H. Lynn tells us that during the Napoleonic wars the

emperors of Russia and France met one night on a raft in the middle of a German river for a conference. That conference was fraught with momentous consequence to millions—a conference to change the map of Europe. But centuries before, one night on a housetop, while the Syrian stars burned brightly in the sky overhead—and while, perhaps, a full moon blossomed like a huge, yellow jonquil in the garden of the stars—there was a greater conference. This was the conference held on a Jerusalem housetop between Jesus and Nicodemus.

We ask:

I. A QUESTION.

What kind of man was Nicodemus? He was a Pharisee— that means he was an orthodox Jew and he believed the Old Testament Scriptures. Yet he had never glimpsed the truth of regeneration as expressed in these Old Testament words:

Then will I sprinkle clean water upon you, and ye shall be clean: from all your filthiness, and from all your idols, will I cleanse you. A new heart also will I give you, and a new spirit will I put within you: and I will take away the stony heart out of your flesh, and I will give you an heart of flesh. And I will put my spirit within you, and cause you to walk in my statutes, and ye shall keep my judgments, and do them (Ezekiel 36:25–27).

He worshiped God according to all the requirements of the Law. He looked for the Messiah. Nicodemus was a ruler of the Jews. That means that he was a member of the Sanhedrin and therefore a man of influence, power, and reputation. No intellectual rill was he among the people, but a river of intelligence in teaching.

Nicodemus was a night disciple—a man of honest questioning and stalemated intellect. On the housetop that night he came one step into the Kingdom. Then he backed off into darkness again. Only after the crucifixion did he throw his cloak of fear into the arms of night and step boldly forth to meet the light.

A man of culture, he!

A man of prayer, he!

A man of undoubted uprightness of character and purity, he!

His life shows us it is possible to love much—and yet mean nothing in matters that matter much and most. His coming to Jesus and going away shows it is possible to be near—yet far. It is possible to know many things, yet know little of the things most worth knowing, the things that matter most in life and death, in time and eternity.

It is possible to conduct reverent inquiry into Christian evidences yet know little of their true force and compulsions. Such a truth the name Nicodemus brings us. Nicodemus was blind—and blind to the fact that he was blind. Nicodemus was ignorant—and ignorant of the fact of his ignorance. Nicodemus was dead—and dead to the fact that he was dead. Nicodemus was lost—and lost to the fact that he was lost. He did not know that unless men are converted and become as little children—not masters in scholarship, not philosophers of the academic grove—they cannot see the Kingdom of God.

While Nicodemus mentioned miracles that night, Jesus spoke of the new birth. And Jesus could not have said more had he called the universe to order. Considering the eight subjects Jesus revealed to Nicodemus, it was as if a cluster of stars had dropped down and moved along to guide a trembling traveler along a lonely road, as if eight gleaming suns had blazed to light one room, as if eight battleships were sent to convoy one drifting canoe.

here is a bridge which nnot be avoided if one is a categorical state- brogated.

...s not a luxury, but a ...e is no avoiding it—*if* ...—*if* we will live right- ...or be unashamed at Kingdom things apart ...perative of the Scrip- ...ic Law were not to be ...ted or rejected at will. ...e ignored at the risk

...oral standards in the ...tial principles that we ...ial examination of the ...e us of the seriousness of the divine imperatives.

Note the following:

". . . this scripture *must* needs have been fulfilled . . ." (Acts 1:16).

The responsibility of governors to dispense justice is not optional but obligatory: "He that ruleth over men *must* be just . . ." (II Samuel 23:3).

The right of the worker to share in the results of his labors is never to be ignored: "The husbandman that laboureth *must* be first partaker of the fruits" (II Timothy 2:6).

Human redemption could be accomplished only by Calvary

suffering: The Son of man *must* suffer (Matthew 16:21).
". . . so *must* the Son of man be lifted up" (John 3:14).

Christ's mediatorial work stands so completely alone as the
only remedy for sin that it cannot be rejected without jeopar-
dizing one's eternal destiny: ". . . there is none other name
under heaven given among men, whereby we *must* be saved"
(Acts 4:12).

There can be no approach to God apart from faith: ". . . he
that cometh to God *must* believe that he is, and that he is a re-
warder of them that diligently seek him" (Hebrews 11:6).

There can be no worship of God without spirituality: ". . .
they that worship him *must* worship him in spirit and in truth"
(John 4:24).

Jesus said: "I *must* be about my Father's business" (Luke
2:49).

And 'tis written: "[Jesus] *must* needs go through Samaria"
(John 4:4).

These and other inspired imperatives emphasize the solem-
nity of that basic "must" to which Jesus gave expression in His
conversation with Nicodemus. Confronted with Christ's decla-
ration, we know that there is only one way to escape from the
dominion of evil, and to enter the Kingdom of God. We *must*
be born again.

W. E. Hardy wrote:

You may study geology and know the earth's rocks, but you
must know the "Rock of Ages." You may study botany plants, their
names, parts, and colors, but you *must* know "The Rose of Sharon
and the Lily of the Valley." You may be a woodsman and know
all the trees of the forest, but you *must* know "The Tree of Life."
You may know animal husbandry, but you *must* know "The Lamb
of God." You may be a great hunter, but you *must* find "The Lion
of the Tribe of Judah." You may eat of the world's best breads,

but you *must* have "The Bread of Life." You may be architects or carpenters and build great houses, but you *must* learn from "The Carpenter of Nazareth." You may sit at the feet of great teachers, or even be one, but you *must* learn from "The Greatest (the Master) Teacher." You may go to the greatest doctors or even be one, but you *must* be cured by "The Great Physician." You may find or possess some of the earth's greatest jewels, but you *must* find and accept "The Pearl of Great Price." You may look at and even know the stars, but you *must* know "The Star of Bethlehem (The Bright and Morning Star)." You may know princes of the earth, but you *must* know "The Prince of Peace." You can even know kings, but you *must* know "The King of kings and Lord of lords." You may have been taken by world conquerors, but you *must* surrender to "The Conqueror of conquerors." You may have your name in many books, but you *must* have your name inscribed in "The Book of Life." You may visit many cities, but you *must* be a citizen of "The New Jerusalem."

Now note:

II. THE FOUNDATION OF THE NEW-BIRTH NECESSITY.

That foundation we find and the reason for the extraordinary mandate we discover when we go back to the Garden of Eden where, in the utter spiritual bankruptcy of the parents of our race we find the reason for Christ's mandatory "Ye *must* be born again." Adam's sin was infidelity—believing Satan rather than God. Adam's sin was prodigious pride—desiring to be like God. Adam's sin was sacrilegious theft—stealing from God that which God reserved to Himself as a token of His sovereignty. Adam's sin was suicide in that it brought them spiritual death. Adam's sin was murder in that he brought death upon all mankind: ". . . by one man sin entered into the world, and death by sin; and so death passed upon all men, for that all have sinned" (Romans 5:12).

In the spiritual death of our first parents, we find a state and nature that can be altered only by the impartation of spiritual life. The depravity that extends to every part of their nature and that is imparted to all of their posterity convinces us of the truth that every son of Adam needs to be reborn.

Adam, the federal head of the race, plunged into sin and carried the whole human race with him. Amid the desolating ruin of Eden's Garden, when Despair pitched his black pavilions upon man's sterile and blasted estate, we learn that being born in sin we *must* be born again—when there was brought about what Chalmers called "the precise deficiency that can only be repaired by regeneration." Death, the death of which he had been solemnly warned, so affected man in his body, soul and spirit that his only salvation consists in a new begetting. He "must be born again." Nothing but regeneration will save this generation. From the king on the throne to the beggar in the gutter, from the highest to the lowest and for all alike, regeneration is the supreme need.

Now let us note:

III. WHAT THE NEW BIRTH IS NOT.

1. *Not church membership.* Joining the church does not bring a new birth any more than putting a parrot in the canary cage gives a parrot the voice of the canary; any more than putting a leper in an art gallery gets rid of leprosy; or a wheel barrow in an automobile factory makes it a Cadillac car. But every born-again one ought to be a church member.

2. *Not baptism.* A man may be baptized under every form of baptism that men call baptism and go an unregenerate way. A man, a Mormon, was baptized four hundred times—"baptized for the dead." Yet that did not save him.

3. *Not partaking of the Lord's Supper.* He may come as a deacon, an elder, a steward, a Christian and come to the Lord's table, after being regular in attendance and punctual in outward practices of the church, and yet not belong to the family of God by the new birth any more than a tramp asked into the king's palace and given a sandwich becomes a member of the royal family.

4. *Not morality.* Morality is good, and greatly to be praised. But morality is as far from regeneration as the planet Mars is from the earth, as the longest distance an archangel could fly in one million years of constantly using his tireless wings. The king on his throne, or being served at his table, having lived an unquestioned life of morality, is as truly unsaved without regeneration as is the ragged, unregenerate derelict in the back alley, seeking food from a garbage can.

Without regeneration you will never pass through heaven's gate. "For in Christ Jesus neither circumcision availeth any thing, nor uncircumcision, but a new creature" (Galatians 6:15).

A preacher asks: "Can it be that an unregenerate church membership has poisoned the blood stream of Christianity until Death grapples at the throat of the church?"

5. *Not reformation.* There is no reformation without regeneration. There can be no real regeneration without reformation. Regeneration is as deep as life, while reformation is an outside matter.

Under conviction of sin, Elizabeth Frye, looking at herself in the mirror, said: "Elizabeth Frye, you are a contemptible small lady—all outside, no inside." Reformation is a garment a man may wear. Regeneration is the life God gives him. Reformation, compared with regeneration, is chaff; regeneration is wheat. Reformation, compared with regeneration, is smoke;

regeneration is fire. Reformation is the shuck; regeneration is the corn. We had as soon try to purify the poisonous water in a well by painting the pump as to try to save people by the white-wash of reformation. Regeneration is not a new *name;* it is a new *nature.*

What is regeneration?

It is a divine change. God does it. "But as many as received him, to them gave he power to become the sons of God, even to them that believe on his name" (John 1:12).

It is *not* generation, or physical birth: ". . . born, not of blood, nor of the will of the flesh, nor of the will of man, but of God" (John 1:13). Without the new birth, Christian children would be Christian because their parents were.

It is *not* education. Education develops the mind, but it does not necessarily develop the soul of man.

It is *not* confirmation. By this we mean a person cannot be born again by merely joining the church, or learning the cate-chism.

Regeneration is *not* "becoming and being better." No. Not being better, but being born—born again. That will guarantee all the "betterness" essential—making it so that a man lives the life in which God is glorified even as the sun is glorified in rare and beautiful flowers.

"O, Lord," muttered Alexander Pope one day, "make me a better man!" "It would be easier," replied his spiritually en-lightened page, "to make you a *new* man." And in that distinc-tion lies the whole doctrine that so startled Nicodemus that night when the words were first spoken.

So the new birth is not the reformation of the outward man, not the education of the natural man, not the purification of the old man, not turning over a new leaf, not mending the manner of life, not "getting religion," not attending church regularly, not participation in church activities, not saying prayers, not reading the Bible. Nor is the new birth morality. Morality is right relations with men. Spirituality is right relations with God. A man may be right with his fellow men who is wrong with God. A man may be all right with his loved ones and all right with his friends and all right with his neighbors who is all wrong with God. And to be wrong with God is tragedy beyond words to describe. Let us note:

IV. WHAT THE NEW BIRTH IS.

Regeneration is the great change which God works in the soul when He brings it into life, when He raises it from the death of sin to the life of righteousness. It is the change wrought when the love of the world is changed into the love of God; when pride is dethroned and humility enthroned; when passion is changed into meekness; when hatred, envy, and malice are changed into a sincere and tender love for all mankind.

It is the change whereby the earthy, sensual, devilish mind is turned into the mind that was in Christ. The new birth is not the old nature altered, reformed, or reinvigorated, but a being born from above.

Dr. Mullins: "When a soul is regenerated, it is changed fundamentally in moral and spiritual quality. The quality it receives is a reproduction in man of the qualities of God. We are made partakers of His divine nature."

Therefore if any man be in Christ, he is a new creature: old things are passed away; behold, all things are become new (II Corinthians 5:17).

Dr. Campbell: "Regeneration involves reclamation, renunciation, repudiation."

The new heart is a complete change, a permanent change. Yes, permanent! A person born from above can never be unborn from below. How can one who has been born ever become unborn? My child may go into the far country and may bring reproach on me, but he is my child—and when he comes to himself he will return.

If we have been born of God we can not wilfully and persistently continue in what we know to be wrong—and, "If we confess our sins, he is faithful and just to forgive us our sins, and to cleanse us from all unrighteousness" (I John 1:9).

A young lady came to her pastor with a statement she had heard the night before. The speaker had said that if the little chickens stay under the mother hen they keep dry, but if they run out from under her feathers when it is raining they get wet. And so those who stay "under the blood" are safe, but they can go out and be lost. The pastor said to the young woman: "If the little chicks run out and get wet, they are still the old hen's chickens. They are just *wet* chickens; they do not become ducks."

Since we know, as many have said, that the natural man has no taste for the things of God, that the carnal mind is enmity against God, that man in his natural and fallen state would not enjoy heaven if he got there, that heaven is a prepared place for a prepared people, we also know that regeneration is the only remedy, and every man must be born again—made a new creature—if he is to see or enter into the Kingdom of God.

In regeneration the dead sinner, the sinner with all the faculties of the soul in moral ruin, is made a child of God, and thus becomes the beneficiary of "the gracious work of God in the human soul by which the heart is enabled to love God, the mind is enabled to understand the gospel of Christ, and the will is brought to choose Christ as both Lord and Saviour." Then, as John Flavel says, the heart which is man's worst part before regeneration and the best part after regeneration, is the seat of principles and the fountain of actions.

Dr. C. D. Cole, of the Toronto Baptist Seminary, teaches that no part of man was annnihilated in the fall, but all parts were ruined or depraved. Therefore, regeneration is not the bringing of any new person into existence, not the bringing of any new faculties into existence. Regeneration is not based upon non-existence, but upon a depraved existence. The unregenerate man has the faculties of mind and heart and will, but they are in a depraved state. With his mind he does not love to think about God and cannot understand the things of God. With his heart the unregenerate man can and does love, but he does not love God. With his will he can and does choose, but he does not choose Christ as Lord and Saviour. In regeneration the direction of man's love, the bent of his affections, and the trend of his will are changed. Thus is the man's affection, once set upon self and sin, set upon God.

We let Dr. Strong illustrate. He speaks of the engineer who climbs over the cab into a runaway locomotive and changes its course. He does not change the course of that locomotive headed for wreck by adding any new part, a new rod or cog, but by simply reversing the lever. So, says Dr. Strong, in regeneration God reverses the lever of the soul, changing man's taste so that a man loves what he once hated and hates what he once loved, feeding upon God's food that once he spurned, thinking things are wise that once he thought foolish, despising things that once gave him delight, evaluating as umbrellas what once he evaluated as solid storm-proof roofs.

The impartation of a new nature, not the eradication of the

sinful nature, is regeneration. The twice-born man has a two-fold disposition or nature. And thus there is in the saved man the conflict between the fleshy and spiritual natures. Paul taught this when he wrote;

For the flesh lusteth against the Spirit, and the Spirit against the flesh: and these are contrary the one to the other: so that ye cannot do the things that ye would (Galatians 5:17).

And Paul had this duel in his dual nature, this assault between the two in his own experience. Paul, delighting in the law of God after the inward man, was conscious of another power. So he testified:

For we know that the law is spiritual: but I am carnal, sold under sin. . . . For the good that I would I do not: but the evil which I would not, that I do. Now if I do that I would not, it is no more I that do it, but sin that dwelleth in me. I find then a law, that, when I would do good, evil is present with me. For I delight in the law of God after the inward man: but I see another law in my members, warring against the law of my mind, and bringing me into captivity to the law of sin which is in my members. O wretched man that I am! who shall deliver me from the body of this death? I thank God through Jesus Christ our Lord. So then with the mind I myself serve the law of God; but with the flesh the law of sin (Romans 7:14, 19–25).

V. NECESSITY OF THE NEW BIRTH.

We do this for re-emphasis.

We do this for amplification.

We do this for illustration—and all for a more comprehensible clarification. We speak not of how man should live but of how and why men are made alive spiritually. A man cannot live before he is born. A dead man cannot regulate his life. For in order to have spiritual discernment, a man must be born again. Until then, he is blind and cannot see the things of God.

But the natural man receiveth not the things of the Spirit of God: for they are foolishness unto him: neither can he know them, because they are spiritually discerned (I Corinthians 2:14).

Unless there be a taste for spiritual things, spiritual surroundings are not happiness. Put a gambler in heaven—would he be happy? No! Put a liquor lover in heaven—will he be happy? No! He will not find a barroom even on the back streets of heaven. Put all who roll sin as a sweet morsel under the tongue— would they be happy in heaven? No! Put a liar in heaven— would he be happy? No!

In his natural birth, born of his mother, man enters the world a sinful creature—estranged from the thrice-holy God. Of all the unregenerate, it is written:

Having the understanding darkened, being alienated from the life of God through the ignorance that is in them, because of the blindness of their heart (Ephesians 4:18).

It is not that the natural man is ignorant and needs instruction, feeble and needs invigorating, sickly and needs doctoring. His case is far more. He is spiritually lifeless, and needs quickening—a spiritual corpse which needs bringing from death to life. This is not an arbitrary decree, but the enunciation of an abiding principle. That which is born of the vegetable is vegetable. That which is born of the animal is animal. That which is born of sinful man is a sinful child. "That which is born of the flesh is flesh." It may be refined and beautiful flesh. But it is flesh. And ". . . flesh and blood cannot inherit the kingdom of God . . ." (I Corinthians 15:50).

So all who live in the flesh in this world must be born into it, for there is no other way of getting into it. All who live in the spiritual world must be born into it, for there is no other way of getting into it. So don't marvel and be astounded that Jesus said, "Ye *must* be born again," or that the Apostle Peter spoke of being born again in these words:

Being born again, not of corruptible seed, but of incorruptible, by the word of God, which liveth and abideth forever (I Peter 1:23).

Being taught that now personal virtues, education, position, and self-righteousness had done all they could for Nicodemus, the ruler of the Jews, and that there was something lacking— and the thing lacking was to be supplied in regeneration—with gratitude I read these wise words from somebody's mind and pen:

A sculptor may take a piece of rough marble and work from it the figure of a Madonna; but it is still nothing but marble, and lifeless. A carver may take a piece of wood, and work out of it a scene of feasting; but it is still wood, and insensible. A watch-cleaner may take a watch, the mainspring of which is broken; he may clean every wheel, cog, pin, hand, face, and the cases; but the mainspring not rectified, it will be as useless for going and time-keeping as before. A poor man may clothe himself in the garb of a monarch; but he is still a poor man. A leper may cover all his spots with his garments; but he is still a leper. So the sinner may reform in all the externals of his life so that he shall attain the moral finery of Saul of Tarsus, or Nicodemus, a master in Israel, but, except he be born again from above, he cannot see the Kingdom of God.

The mighty and majestic Moody, who took a continent in his left hand and another continent in his right hand and rocked them both toward God, said, preaching of the necessity of the new birth:

You may see many countries; but there is one country, the land of Beulah, which John Bunyan saw in vision, you shall never behold, unless you are born again—regenerated by Christ. You can look ahead and see many beautiful trees, but the tree of life you shall never behold unless your eyes are clear by faith in the Saviour. You may see the beautiful rivers of earth, you may ride upon their bosoms, but bear in mind that your eyes will never rest upon the river which bursts out from the Throne of God and flows through the upper Kingdom, unless you are born again. You may see the kings and lords of earth; but the King of kings and the Lord of lords you will never see unless you are born again.

When you are in London, you may go to the Tower and see the crown of England, which is worth thousands of pounds, and is guarded there by soldiers, but bear in mind that your eye will never rest upon the crown of life except you are born again. You may hear the songs of Zion which are sung here; but one song— that of Moses and the Lamb—the uncircumcised ear will never hear; its melody will only gladden the ears of those who have been born again. You may look upon the beautiful mansions of the earth; but bear in mind that the mansions which Christ has gone to prepare you shall never see unless you are born again.

It is God who says it. You may see ten thousand beautiful things in this world; but the city that Abraham caught a glimpse of—and from that time became a pilgrim and sojourner—you shall never see unless you are born again (Hebrews 11:8, 11–13). Many of you may be invited to marriage feasts here; but you will never attend the marriage supper of the Lamb except you are born again.

The necessity of the new birth is shown in that the human heart is "deceitful above all things and desperately wicked" (Jeremiah 17:9), is affected with a malady which no example can cure, no philosophy can change, no ritualistic formulas or religious ceremonies can reach and change.

I repeat, the natural man, in his unregenerate state, cannot understand the things of the Spirit (I Corinthians 2:14). He is blind (II Corinthians 4:4); he is dead in trespasses and sins (Ephesians 2:1–3); his understanding is darkened (Ephesians 4:18–19); full of evil thoughts (Genesis 6:5, Jeremiah 17:9), and unable to please God (Romans 8:8).

Therefore, as all who believe the Word of God know, a new birth, even a birth from above, is needed because of the depravity of human nature.

Man is not born physically with qualities that please God. "So then they that are in the flesh cannot please God" (Romans 8:8).

Paul, with wisdom far beyond the preaching of those who say that all men are children of God, reminds the Jews that being the fleshly descendents of Abraham did not make them children of God (Romans 9:8). Knowing ourselves, we know that man has the inherited corruption of a fallen nature. Dr. Cole said that David was not casting reflection upon his mother's virtue, but was confessing to inborn depravity, when he exclaimed: "Behold, I was shapen in iniquity; and in sin did my mother conceive me" (Psalm 51:5). Christ taught that the human heart was the very fountain of all that is sinful:

For from within, out of the heart of men, proceed evil thoughts, adulteries, fornications, murders, thefts, covetousness, wickedness, deceit, lasciviousness, an evil eye, blasphemy, pride, foolishness: All these evil things come from within, and defile the man (Mark 7:21–23).

God's will should be supreme in every life, but the human will is antagonistic to God—and man by nature is dominated by self-will. "All we like sheep have gone astray; we have turned everyone to his own way . . ." (Isaiah 53:6). There must be a spiritual birth before there can be spiritual understanding.

I read in "The Gospel Witness" of a little girl with a defect of vision from her birth. Her parents were slow to realize that she could not see many objects which were familiar to others. She was almost grown before an occulist was consulted. He advised and performed an operation, and the child was kept in a dark room for many weeks. One bright and balmy night she stepped out alone upon the lawn. Instantly she rushed back into the house in a glow of excitement. "Oh, come," she cried, "and see what has happened to the sky!" Her parents hurried out with her, but they saw nothing but the glory of the stars—something the child had never seen before. Nothing had happened to the sky, but something had happened to her eyes. So the unregenerate man has the eyes of his understanding darkened in respect to spiritual and saving truth. The stars of gospel truth shine brightly in the firmament of the Word of God, but the lost man does not see them. "But if our Gospel be hid, it is hid to them that are lost" (II Corinthians 4:4). The trouble then is with the sinner's darkened understanding. There is nothing wrong with the truth—and truth does not need "energizing" or "illuminating." God does not make the truth more true any more than He makes one truth truer than another truth. But God opens sin-blinded minds to *understand* the truth (I Corinthians 3:5; II Corinthians 4:6). And thus, convinced in his *mind* of the truth about Jesus and of the truth that Jesus is *the* Truth, a sinner is brought "Out of his bondage, sorrow, and night, into Christ's freedom, gladness, and light." "Ye shall know the truth, and the truth shall make you free" (John 8: 32). And thus, convicted in his heart that he is a lost sinner, hell-doomed and hell-deserving, the transgressor is brought "out of his sin-sickness into Christ's health," out of his poverty and bankruptcy into Christ's wealth.

And thus, committing his personal will to the personal truth in Christ and to the will of Christ, the lost sinner is brought "out of his shameful failure and loss into the glorious gain of Christ's cross"—rejoicing in this prayerful statement of Jesus:

And this is life eternal, that they might know thee the only true God, and Jesus Christ whom thou hast sent (John 17:3).

And thus we see that a man *can* be born again when he is old, showing that the best proof of Christianity is a Christian, giving evidence that the best proof of regeneration is a man who has been regenerated.

Think of Jerry McCauley, the river-wharf thief, and Jerry McCauley, the servant of God in the slums.

Think of Mel Trotter, the stupid rum-soaked loafer and Mel Trotter, the rescuer of those who had fallen into sin's sewerage gutters.

Think of Sam Jones, the whiskey-blighted lawyer, who became a peddler of cabbages, and Sam Jones, the flaming and fearless evangelist of God who pointed hundreds of thousands to the Lamb of God.

Think of Ernest Reveal, once crippled in sin, and Ernest Reveal, the spiritual athlete for God, keeping a gospel lamp burning brightly for forty-two years in Evansville, Indiana, breaking, with the help of God, the fetters of booze from the lives of many.

Think of Pat Withrow, wrecked by Satan and worthless for God, and Pat Withrow, as one who delivered himself, delivered many others from dungeons of despair.

Think of B. H. Carroll, the infidel and B. H. Carroll, the theological giant, Bible expositor and founder of a great seminary.

It was Henry Drummond, saved as a cultured college professor, who wrote: "Think of Bunyan the sinner and Bunyan, the saint; think of Newton the miscreant and Newton the missionary; think of Paul the persecutor and Paul the apostle; and *marvel not,* as if it were impossible that a man should be born again."

Let us think now of:

VI. THE CAUSE OF THE NEW BIRTH.

When Marie Antoinette left Vienna for Paris to become the wife of the king, she proceeded as far as Kell on the French frontier in her own gorgeous garments and with her own retinue of attendants. But, at Kell, she found a building erected on the border where she must undergo the ceremonies of leaving all that was Austrian behind and taking up all that was French for the future. One end of the apartment, on the Austrian side, was for the lord and ladies of Vienna. In her own private apartment she was unrobed of all her garments and the door opening to the French side was thrown open while this beautiful and blushing child advanced. The French ladies rushed to meet her. Marie threw herself into the arms of the Countess de Novilles. "The French were perfectly enchanted with her beauty. The proud position of her head and shoulders betrayed to their eyes the daughter of the Caesars."

She was then re-dressed in the best that the French monarchy had. However good the Austrian garments, she could not be admitted to the French court in anything except French clothing, because it was the law of the land.

When Paul passed from the kingdom of darkness to the kingdom of light, having put away the old garments, he found himself arrayed for admission to the court of heaven in the glorious garments of Christ's righteousness.

My hope is built on nothing less
Than Jesus' blood and righteousness.

No one can ever be admitted to the Kingdom of God without the righteousness which is by faith.

But how is this admittance to the Kingdom of God brought about? What is the manner of the new birth? Let us note three things:

1. *The Will of God.*

But as many as received him, to them gave he power to become the sons of God, even to them that believe on his name: Which were born, not of blood, nor of the will of the flesh, nor of the will of man, but of God (John 1:12–13).

Of his own will begat he us with the word of truth, that we should be a kind of firstfruits of his creatures (James 1:18).

2. *The Word of God.*

God's Word gives guidance and shows the way of life, the way of heaven. God's Word is final. Listen:

Forasmuch as ye know that ye were not redeemed with corruptible things, as silver and gold, from your vain conversation received by tradition from your fathers; But with the precious blood of Christ, as of a lamb without blemish and without spot. . . . Being born again, not of corruptible seed, but of incorruptible, by the word of God, which liveth and abideth for ever (I Peter 1:18–19, 23).

3. *By the Holy Spirit of God.*

That which is born of the flesh is flesh; and that which is born of the Spirit is spirit (John 3:6).

The subjects of the spiritual kingdom must enter that kingdom by spiritual birth, since flesh and blood cannot inherit the Kingdom of God (I Corinthians 15:50). According to the law of generation, like produces like; flesh produces flesh, and spirit alone can produce spirit:

Not by works of righteousness which we have done, but according to his mercy he saved us, by the washing of regeneration, and renewing of the Holy Ghost; Which he shed on us abundantly through Jesus Christ our Saviour (Titus 3:5–6).

"The Word gives *knowledge* of spiritual things; the Holy Spirit gives *capacity* for spiritual things. The gospel is *objective* light; the Holy Spirit gives *subjective* light."

The new birth is a spiritual process, a spiritual experience, a supernatural work of God, wrought in the hearts of those who come in humility, confessing their sins and their inability to save themselves and accepting in faith the work which our Saviour, the eternal Son of God, has done for us. Thus do we see the truth of being born of the Spirit; thus do we see that the agency is the Holy Spirit. As one has said, the power of the Holy Spirit is immediate, that is, the Spirit does not flow through anything, not even the gospel itself. The gospel is hated and rejected as foolishness until the direct power of the Spirit changes the governing disposition of the heart. I quote these words by one whose name I have forgotten:

Our natural hearts are hearts of stone. The Word of God is good seed sown on the hard, trodden, macadamized highway, which the horses of passion, the asses of self-will, the wagons of imaginary treasure, have made impenetrable. Only the Holy Spirit can soften and pulverize the soil. The gospel is good seed, but good seed cannot make good soil. Paul may plant and Apollos may water, but God must give the increase.

And now, with prayerful conclusion, we would speak:

VIII. WORDS OF WARNING.

"Ye *must* be born again."

There is no detour, though many have been attempted.
Writes a wise man:

Time, effort and money are directed into an educational program which seeks to detour around the new birth. The same can
be said for multiplied efforts to change the environmental circum-
stances of individuals, especially the less fortunate. There are
multiplied activities to change the personal outlook of individuals
toward the social problems of our day, ignoring the sobering fact
that until a man is born again he will never become a truly ad-
justed personality himself, nor can he make his rightful contribution to the social needs of his generation.

"Born . . . of God." Nothing short of that will suffice. It is
God's part to create and bestow life. It is man's part to believe
on Him (John 1:12–13). Christ is the Mediator between God
and man (I Timothy 2:5). He is the One whose death made
new life possible. Believing upon Him and accepting for ourselves His work of dying, His payment of our sin debt, His sacrifice of bearing our sins "in his own body on the tree" (I Peter
2:24), we shall be pardoned, justified, given a new nature from
that which we have now (II Peter 2:14). To know Christ is to
have eternal life (John 17:3).

But as we rejoice in that truth, we would give a warning. We
do so in the words of Dwight L. Moody:

If you are not sure that you have become a partaker of the
Divine nature, don't eat, drink or sleep until you are. And when
you get that new nature, it is easy to serve God: His yoke is easy,
His burden is light (Matthew 11:30). O man, woman, you may be

deceived about ten thousand things, but *do not be deceived on this one thing*. Make sure that you have been born from above, born of God—a life distinct and separate from the natural life—a new life, a new creation.

This is an awfully solemn question. Put it now to ourselves: "Have I been born again? Have I received the gift of God, which is eternal life?" Father, mother, perhaps you have not a hope in Jesus Christ. That little child that left you a few months ago lived long enough to twine itself around your heart; then death came and took that little child into a brighter and better world; you will never see that child again except you are born of God. O man, woman, be wise, be wise now; make sure you get into the Kingdom of God!

4 Wanted: More Funerals

. . . the Lord smote Nabal, that he died. And when David heard that Nabal was dead, he said, Blessed be the Lord . . . (I Samuel 25:38–39).

Therefore thus saith the Lord concerning Jehoiakim the son of Josiah king of Judah; They shall not lament for him, saying, Ah my Brother! or, Ah sister! they shall not lament for him, saying, Ah lord! or, Ah his glory! He shall be buried with the burial of an ass, drawn and cast forth beyond the gates of Jerusalem (Jeremiah 22:18–19).

I would have you think of:

I. SOME BURIALS.

Sarah, Abraham's wife, died at one hundred and twenty-seven years of age in Hebron, in the land of Canaan. And ". . . Abraham came to mourn for Sarah and to weep for her" (Genesis 23:2). No pleasure was it to him to bury her in the cave of Machpelah.

Abraham died at one hundred and seventy-five years of age (Genesis 25:7). Isaac and Ishmael found no pleasure in burying him in the cave of Machpelah—beside Sarah.

Isaac died at one hundred and eighty years of age (Genesis 35:28).

And Esau and Jacob saw shadows in the sunlight of that day —when they put him to rest on earth's couch of clay.

When Jacob came to the sunset gates, as one glad to lay all of life's burdens down, he made this request of his sons: ". . . bury me with my fathers in the cave that is in the field of Ephron the Hittite" (Genesis 49:29).

There they buried Abraham and Sarah his wife; there they buried Isaac and Rebekah his wife; and there I buried Leah (Genesis 49:31).

But no pleasure had Joseph in the burial of his father. We read: "And Joseph fell upon his father's face, and wept upon him, and kissed him" (Genesis 50:1).

Joseph, in his lifetime, with his faith in God manifesting itself in great statesmanship, wiped frowns of foreboding from King Pharaoh's face and took famine fear from the heart of the whole nation. And sadness, sombre as a dark cloud, covered the land when he died. Many felt like weeping when "they embalmed him [Joseph], and he was put in a coffin in Egypt" (Genesis 50:26).

When Moses, a mighty Matterhorn in the history of God's chosen people, died at one hundred and twenty years of age, "his eye was not dim, nor his natural force abated," ". . . the children of Israel wept for Moses in the plains of Moab thirty days . . ." (Deuteronomy 34:8).

Joshua, with many battles fought and many victories won, known as servant of the Lord died (Joshua 24:29). There was no joy when they digged his grave and buried him ". . . on the north side of the hill of Gaash" (Joshua 24:30).

Samson, who after he had judged Israel twenty years, was lured to destruction by devilish Delilah, died with the Philistines amid the wreckage of the house.

Then his brethren and all the house of his father came down and took him, and brought him up, and buried him . . . in the buryingplace of Manoah his father (Judges 16:31).

But to those who buried him, the birds that sang that day seemed to wail.

Think of Samuel, who washed the heart of Israel with the snow of high ideals, who walked in righteousness before the people from his childhood to his old age:

And Samuel died; and all the Israelites were gathered together, and lamented him, and buried him in his house at Ramah. And David arose, and went down to the wilderness of Paran (I Samuel 25:1).

King Saul, first king of Israel, began like a mighty river for good and ended like a feeble rill, died a wretched suicide on Mt. Gilboa.

And sad were they all: "All the valiant men arose, and went all night, and took the body of Saul" and buried it (I Samuel 31: 12–13). And the expression "fasted seven days" showed that they found no pleasure in Saul's death.

Abner, adored by some, abominable to others, died, King David himself following the bier:

And they buried Abner in Hebron: and the king lifted up his voice, and wept at the grave of Abner; and all the people wept. And the king lamented over Abner, and said, Died Abner as a fool dieth? (II Samuel 3:32–33).

That day multitudes wept.

Wild, wayward, wicked, handsome Absalom died.

And the king was much moved, and went up to the chamber over the gate, and wept: and as he went, thus he said, O my son Absalom, my son, my son Absalom! would God I had died for thee, O Absalom, my son, my son! (II Samuel 18:33).

King David served his day and generation by the will of God. "And he died in a good old age, full of days, riches, and honour: and Solomon his son reigned in his stead" (I Chronicles 29:28). And many had sorrow because a funeral was a necessity.

At Joppa, Dorcas, a woman "full of good works and almsdeeds which she did," died. The disciples sent to Lydda for the Apostle Peter, ". . . desiring him that he would not delay to come to them." We read:

Then Peter arose and went with them. When he was come, they brought him into the upper chamber: and all the widows stood by him weeping, and shewing the coats and garments which Dorcas made, while she was with them (Acts 9:39).

Sad were all when Dorcas died. Glad were all when Dorcas was brought to life.

But when God smote churlish, selfish, drunken Nabal "that he died," David said: "Blessed be the Lord who hath pleaded the cause of my reproach from the hand of Nabal" (I Samuel 25:39).

Yes, because of a funeral David said: "Blessed be the Lord!"

Jehoiakim, wicked son of good King Jehosephat, died. And concerning his death and burial we read:

Therefore thus saith the Lord concerning Jehoiakim the son of Josiah king of Judah; They shall not lament for him, saying, Ah my brother! or, Ah sister! they shall not lament for him, saying, Ah lord! or, Ah his glory! He shall be buried with the burial of an ass, drawn and cast forth beyond the gates of Jerusalem (Jeremiah 22:18–19).

And when Haman was hanged on the gallows he had prepared for Mordecai, ". . . Then was the king's wrath pacified" (Esther 7:10). "The Jews had . . . gladness . . ." (Esther 8:16).

Rejoicing, not regret, was in the hearts of many. Terrible it is for a man to live so wickedly that people will be glad to hear that he "has shuffled off this mortal coil."

Tragic it is for a woman to live so selfishly and wickedly that people find pleasure in reading her obituary.

Once I knew a man, yea, I conducted his funeral. At the funeral a neighbor said: "Now his wife will have some peace and his little children some happiness."

Think just a little of:

II. MY MINISTRY AND FUNERALS.

I love to work.

I love to lighten loads for people.

I love to brighten roads for people.

But if there is ever a time when I go even with reluctance and never with rejoicing it is when I conduct funeral services. Sometimes there is more crepe on my mind than was ever placed on a doorway. A physical depletion and a mental disturbance which I cannot explain comes to me when I minister beside the coffin and at the grave. Conducting funerals is the most sorrowful service of my ministry—unless it be when I try to salvage the wrecks of matrimonial ships. There is seldom a week that passes but that funerals cast shadows on my pathway. It is good to bring comfort to grief-stricken hearts, to tell people that God ". . . redeemeth the soul of his servants: and none of them that trust in him shall be desolate" (Psalm 34:22). But I live painfully amid funeral surges of emotion until exhaustion assaults me often, though I may show no signs of such. At funerals, the roll of the hearse wheels holds no music for my ears. The sunshine of funeral days holds shadows for me. The rain that falls on funeral days is the dreariest of all rains to me. The tears I see sometimes fall like hammer strokes on my heart. Sobs I hear smite my ear drums like thunders of discord. Dead faces and faces drenched with tears often appear before me in my dreams the night after I have conducted funerals.

Yet there are some funerals I would like to conduct, some burials that would give me joy. I mention a few.

I would find joy in conducting the funeral of:

A. *Mr. and Mrs. Jealousy.*

In the Bible we read: ". . . jealousy is cruel as the grave; the coals thereof are coals of fire . . ." (Song of Solomon 8:6). "For jealousy is the rage of a man" (Proverbs 6:34).

The brothers of Joseph had jealousy of the most destructive type.

And when his brethren saw that their father loved him more than all his brethren, they hated him, and could not speak peaceably unto him (Genesis 37:4).

David was the victim of Saul's jealousy.

And the women answered one another as they played, and said, Saul hath slain his thousands, and David his ten thousands. And Saul was very wroth and the saying displeased him; and he said, They have ascribed unto David ten thousands, and to me they have ascribed but thousands: and what can he have more but the kingdom? And Saul eyed David from that day forward (I Samuel 18:7–9).

After the prodigal son returned from the far country, his father sponsored a big banquet reception. But the elder brother became jealous: "And he was angry and would not go in . . ." (Luke 15:28).

Jealousy is essentially selfish. It calls for all successes, all compliments, all advantages, all accomplishments—everything to be for itself.

Dr. Riley said: "Let no man conclude that divine favor and God's use of a man will insure against human hatred. Jealousy is the blindest of passions. Jealousy never sees anything except through green glasses which convert all virtues into vice."

Because this is one of the most prevalent vices of the world today, because many are victims of this green-eyed monster, because jealousy is cruel as the grave, I could, with joy, conduct the funeral for the whole jealousy family, seeing that jealousy is evil continually.

Because of jealousy, Cain slew Abel. Because of jealousy, Miriam criticized Moses. Because of jealousy, King Saul sought to slay David. Because of jealousy, Joseph's brethren sold him into slavery. Because of jealousy, Christ's enemies sent him to the cross.

The havoc wrought by jealousy, no one can estimate. The story of jealousy between and among nations is written in letters of blood and fire across all the pages of history. Jealousy poisons our social relations, our political relations, our religious relations. And what a devastating despoiler it is of domestic relations. Daily, homes intended to be a foretaste of heaven are turned into vestibules of hell by the demon of jealousy. Jealousy is the vandal in the house of love. Because of jealousy's slaying of people—their peace of mind, their rectitude, their reputation—I could with gladness and gratitude conduct its funeral.

Another funeral needed and wanted is the funeral of:

B. *Misses Gossip and Scandal.*

They are the twin daughters of Mr. and Mrs. Jealousy. I know this because Jealousy and Envy are parents of most of the evil speaking and slandering that pollutes the world.

Clarence Darrow once said: "I've never murdered a man, but I have read many an obituary with pleasure." So say I about the Misses Gossip and Scandal—because they are ". . . full of envy, murder, debate, deceit, malignity; whisperers" (Romans 1:29).

Their whispers, going into any ear that will listen, are like the hiss of the serpent as it projects its venom. Gossip and Scandal are responsible for miseries immeasurable and deserve the holy anathema and execration of all Christians.

Talmage describes them in these words: "They are to be found everywhere. They have a prying disposition. They can see as far through a keyhole as other people can see with a door wide open. They can hear conversation on the opposite side of the room. They put the worst construction on everything. Set on fire of this hellish spirit, they keep the whole neighborhood abroil."

Gossip works all sorts of misery and mischief. Yet folks speak of *idle* gossip.

But about the busiest, fastest-moving thing on earth is what folks call idle rumor. It works overtime. It works fast. It works without any weariness. It works without ever taking a vacation. Bob Burns said: "Three of the fastest spreading things I know of are poison ivy, devil's grass, and gossip." Yes, gossip works fast. Somebody else said: "A gossip in a village is like a viper in a bed."

As to these Misses Gossip and all the Gossip family, if you

shut them off from one route of perfidy, they start on another. It seems that nothing can stop them—except the cutting out of their tongues. I think it was Sterne who spoke of them as a pestilence which levels without distinction the good and the bad. Another reminds us that gossip, like the Nile, is fed by innumerable streams, but it is extremely difficult to trace it to its source. And we might remember with profit the warning of Alfred Henry Lewis: "In scandal, as in robbery, the receiver is always as bad as the thief."

Frank Pratt, a writer of Columbus, Miss., wrote: "I am not an authority on hell. What I think about the matter will not change the program one bit. But the one thing that convinces me there is a hell is that there is no other place for gossips to go. I fear even then hell, in all its fury, will fail to do justice when they arrive."

It is doubtful if anything is so destructive of happiness as words of gossips and scandal mongers. Someone has reminded us that it is recorded in the Gospels that when Christ gave a dumb man speech, Christ sighed. For he probably reflected that this man might do more mischief with his tongue in five minutes than he could undo in a lifetime.

> Boys flying kites, haul in their white-winged birds
> You can't do that way when you are flying words.
> Thoughts that we think may sometimes fall back dead,
> But God Himself can't kill them when they're said.

All members of the Gossip family talk, talk, talk. They have the good names of many they leave looking like a barnyard after it has been trampled by animals, after the foxes and weasles have been around—"here a claw, yonder an eye, there a pile of feathers."

Before people gossip and spread rumors about any human being, they should ask three questions. First: Is it true? Take pains to find out before you speak. Second: Is it kind? Make sure of that. Third: Is it necessary? Remember reputation is like a mirror—a blow will crush it, a breath will blur it. Therefore, ask: Is it true? Is it kind? Is it necessary?

I think it was Dr. Talmage who said: "Rather than the defamation of good names it would be more honorable if you took a box of matches in your pocket and a razor in your hand—and would go around seeing how many houses you can burn down and how many throats you can cut. The destruction of a man's name is worse than the destruction of his life."

An ancient writer says that a slanderer and a man who receives the slander ought both to be hung—the one by the tongue, the other by the ear. Do not retail whispers and slander. Do not make yourself the inspector of warts—the supervisor of carbuncles—the inspector of gutters—the weed noticer in a man's life garden.

With joy and gratitude, I could officiate at the funeral of Gossip and Scandal, be gossip masculine or feminine.

We need to remember what James Whitcomb Riley wrote:

> When over the fair fame of friend or foe
>   The shadow of disgrace shall fall; instead
> Of words of blame, or proof of so and so,
>   Let something good be said.
>
> Forget not that no fellow-being yet
>   May fall so low but love may lift his head;
> Even the cheek of shame with tears is wet,
>   Let something good be said.
>
> No generous heart may vainly turn aside
>   In ways of sympathy; no soul so dead

But may awaken strong and glorified,
  If something good be said.

And so I charge ye, by the thorny crown,
  And by the cross on which the Saviour bled,
And by your own soul's hope for fair renown,
  Let something good be said.

Another funeral I would be glad to conduct is the funeral of:

C. Resentment and Retaliation.

The funeral of Mr. Resentment and Mr. Retaliation would be a joy to me, a great joy. At such a funeral I could laugh. I would say: Blessed the shroud that enfolds him, blessed the coffin that encases him, blessed the funeral men who bury him, blessed the hole in the ground that holds him. May no tombstone be placed to hold him in memory. May no flowers bloom where he sleeps. May grass high hide his resting place. May resurrection be denied him.

So many people feel that they have a right to harbor hard feelings against one who has hurt their feelings, or otherwise injured them. So many believe they have a right to be resentful because their ideas were not given rushing acceptance, because they could not have their way in matters, because their opinions were not accepted as commands by others, as orders from superiors.

It is a good thing to bear in mind that those who cherish a grievance and give rein to the spirit of resentment, harness themselves far more than they do the object of their wrath. Instead of spending fruitless time brooding over your wounds or waiting for a chance to get even, spend your time in getting ahead.

Be like Ole Bull. When told that another musician and some newspapers were saying bitter things against him, he said: "They talk against me; I play against them."

It has been truly said that the lower you go in the scale of being, the more you find the spirit of retaliation. Go down from man and you come at length to the hornet and the rattlesnake. You hurt them, they hurt you. Go up from man through whatever grades of beings there may be above us and at last you come to the throne of God. And there you find nothing but love —wounded love it may be, crucified love, but always love— the very love that from the cross cried out, "Father, forgive them, for they know not what they do."

The weapon Christ would put in your hand wherewith to slay the demon of resentment is *pity*. If you knew all about the life of your worst enemy, you would pity him—and, if you want to be like Christ, forgive him. So instead of feeding resentment until it becomes a giant that cannot be controlled, sentence it to speedy death with the weapon of pity. And I shall be pleased to be there and to have a part in the funeral—and to recite the Lord's prayer.

I would also like to conduct the funeral of:

D. Mr. Snarler.

I could, with gratitude beyond words to express, conduct the funeral of Snarlism. I do not wish for any snarler at Christianity to die—not even a Russian leader, not even an infidel. But I think I should give herewith an editorial entitled "The Snarler" by Dr. Bob Shuler:

I know a young businessman who seems to pride himself on his cynicism and critical attitude toward Christianity. A few years ago a boy worked for him. Later that boy became a young minister. Now, whenever the two meet, this young businessman delights in making dirty digs and vicious thrusts at this boy's religion, accusing him of trying to dead-beat his way through life, etc.

This young businessman has been represented to me as being an atheist. He is possibly an agnostic. He has nothing to do with the church. He gives no support to Christianity. He is antagonistic in his attitude to the Christian religion. He is more than a scoffer. He is a snarler.

Some time ago the boy in question happened to be talking with me and asked me what I thought of this young businessman. I am not answering his question. But I will tell my readers what this young businessman would think of any other man who had received the benefits that he has received from Christianity, and who in return took the attitude that he takes toward those factors that have so largely contributed to his life. He would consider him an ingrate.

The young businessman in question is rearing a small family. I do not hesitate to say that he would not rear that family in a town which boasted that it had no churches and that it did not permit the gospel of Jesus Christ to be preached within its borders. He would move elsewhere, even at a financial loss. His business holdings would decrease fifty cents on the dollar, should the town where he has them banish churches and preachers and advertise itself a community of agnostics and atheists. The fact is, he is riding without paying his fare. From a standpoint of his relation to the Christian religion and the civilization that it has fostered and seeks to maintain, he is a sponger!

This young cynic who accuses preachers of being grafters and moochers had a Christian mother. He got his education in the public schools which, if he would take time to go back historically to the facts, was the direct product of the activities of the church. He grew up in America, which is acknowledgedly the beneficiary of Christianity as no other nation on earth. There is no way to compute the direct and indirect benefits that he has received from Christianity. If he actually wants to be an atheist or an agnostic, why does he not seek out a nation like Russia and make his home there? There he would have plenty of company in his hate of preachers and Christianity. . . .

Would he be sincere and honest enough, should his wife or one of his children die, to refuse to have a Christian funeral? If he knew that he was near death, would he ask his wife to see to it that no minister conducted services over his remains?

To scoff and snarl at Christianity is no light thing. Any man who does so marks himself as ridiculing the force that has done more to lift humanity and enlighten the world than all other forces combined. All any man need do to ascertain the facts is to read history. There are only two excuses for such an antagonistic attitude: gross ignorance and unadulterated meanness!

Another funeral I could conduct with abundant joy and immeasurable gratitude would be the funeral of:

E. Old John Barleycorn.

That old rascal! I have more respect for a rattlesnake on a children's playground than I have for him. I can say nicer things about embezzlers and rapists than I can say about him—because I know that ". . . strong drink is raging: and whosoever is deceived thereby is not wise" (Proverbs 20:1)—because I know that it is the source of great sorrows, wounds without cause, cruel contentions, and "At the last it biteth like a serpent, and stingeth like an adder" (Proverbs 23:32).

And if in the funeral sermon I expressed all I feel about him, I would talk for days and days. His funeral would be as welcome to me as an election to a doubtful candidate. The old liar! His funeral would be as welcome to me as fried chicken to hungry preachers. The old hoary hypocrite! His funeral to me would be as welcome as a watermelon to a Negro. The old devil! His funeral would be as welcome to me as a husband to a lady who

has long sought a husband. The old deceiver! His funeral would
be as welcome to me as home to a sailor after a stormy voyage.
The old robber and bandit! How I would like to dig him a grave
a mile deep and write his epitaph in words of condemnation!

Look what that old liar and mighty and merciless miscreant
has done. He causes fathers to damn their own children. He
divides families. He causes men to make their marriage vows
perjury. He is powerful, aggressive and universal in his attack.

Henry Grady says:

Tonight he enters a humble home to strike the roses from a
woman's cheek and tomorrow he challenges this Republic in the
halls of Congress. Today he strikes the crust from the lips of a
starving child, and tomorrow levies tribute from the government
itself. There is no cottage in this city humble enough to escape
him—no palace strong enough to shut him out. He defies the law
when it cannot coerce suffrage. He is flexible to cajole, but merciless in victory. He is the mortal enemy of peace and order, the
despoiler of men, the terror of women, the cloud that shadows the
face of children, the demon that has dug more graves and sent
more souls unshriven to judgment than all the pestilences that
have wasted life since God sent the plagues to Egypt and all the
wars since Joshua stood before Jericho.

It comes to bring gray-haired mothers down in sorrow to their
graves. It comes to turn the wife's love into despair, and her pride
into shame. It comes to still the laughter on the lips of little children and to stifle all the music of the home and fill it with silence
and desolation. It comes to ruin your body and mind, to wreck
your home, and it measures the duration of its prosperity by the
swiftness and certainty with which it does its work.

Intoxicating beverages never touched an individual that it
did not leave upon him an indelible stain. It never touched a
family that it did not plant the seeds of misery and dissolution.
It never touched a community that it did not lower the moral

tone, chill religion and undermine law. It never touched a state that it did not multiply crime, destroy wealth and increase the burdens of taxation. It never touched a nation that it did not clog the machinery of government, blight prosperity, weaken patriotism and encourage treason.

Old John Barleycorn is against the *individual*. I would like to weave his shroud. Old John Barleycorn is against the *home*. I would like to dig his grave. Old John Barleycorn is against the *school*. I would like to build his coffin. Old John Barleycorn is against the *church*. I would like to screw the coffin lid over his face. Old John Barleycorn is against the *nation*. I would like to make him a feast for buzzards. Old John Barleycorn is against the *world*. I would like to put a mountain of stone over his grave. Old John Barleycorn is against the *Kingdom of God*. I would like to have all you serve as active and honorary pallbearers.

They shall not drink wine with a song; strong drink shall be bitter to them that drink it (Isaiah 24:9).

But they also have erred through wine, and through strong drink are out of the way; the priest and the prophet have erred through strong drink, they are swallowed up of wine, they are out of the way through strong drink; they err in vision, they stumble in judgment (Isaiah 28:7).

Nobody can truthfully deny that strong drink destroys life, squanders property, debases character, injures health, mars happiness, corrupts the State, incites to crime, spoils home life, ruins souls—an enemy that enters the mouths and stomachs of men to steal away their brains.

Dr. Haldane of Cambridge University has said: "A man is about five times as likely to get cancer if he drinks beer daily and no milk, as if he drinks milk daily and no beer."

Another funeral I would like to conduct is the funeral of:

F. Worry.

I would like to bury Mr. Worry and Mrs. Worry and all the Worry family in one grave.

In my reading, I have learned that wise men look upon worry and have described worry as a bootlegger of trouble, as an illegitimate child of ambition, as a spiritual bandit who steals your peace of mind, as a common thief who snatches the fruit of the most hard-earned victory.

Worry begins in an honest solicitude and, fattening on trouble, becomes a relentless monster. Worry compels us to cross bridges that were never built over chasms that never existed. Worry compels us to fight battles with phantom antagonists. Worry compels us to prepare for dangers that fade away before we get to them. Look at the faces about you and notice the scars left there by conflicts and sorrow. Worry and imagination are the Siamese twins—twin foes—of tranquility and efficiency. Can you do a better day's work by worrying all the night before? Can you pass a better examination by worrying about it? Does worry help you write an editorial? Patch a tire? Preach a sermon? Teach a Sunday school lesson? Settle a quarrel or escape illness?

Dr. Theodore L. Cuyler wrote about worry, saying:

Worry is not only a sin against God, it is a sin against ourselves. Thousands have shortened their lives by it, and millions have made their lives bitter by dropping this gall into their souls every day. Honest work very seldom hurts us; it is worry that kills. I have a perfect right to ask God for strength equal to the day, but I have no right to ask Him for one extra ounce of strength for tomorrow's burden. When tomorrow comes grace will come with it, and sufficient for the tasks, the trial, or the troubles. God has never built a Christian strong enough to stand the strain of present duties and all the tons of tomorrow's duties and sufferings piled upon the top of him.

And Emerson wrote: "Some of your hurts you have cured and the sharpest you still have survived. But what torments of grief you endured from evils that never arrived."

It does not pay to worry about the weather; you can't change it. About your neighbors; they don't appreciate it. About your business; it isn't worth it. About your money; that's a small matter. About your insults; they can't hurt you. About your landlord; he will remember you anyhow—no matter anything or anybody.

The more we worry about health, the higher the doctor bills will be. The more we worry about mistakes, the more certain we are to make them. The more we worry about luck, the more certain we are to have hard luck. The more we worry about bad weather, the less we enjoy good weather. The more we worry about work, the less fitted we are to do our best. The more we worry about the cost of clothes, the less time we have for mental growth. The more we worry about imaginary troubles, the less able we are to meet real ones.

Why worry about heaven if you are seeing God here? Why worry about money if it only causes us more worry? Why worry about friends if those friends laugh at your convictions? Why worry about a mansion if you are not living right in a cottage? Why worry about criticism when you know any fly can find a sore, any buzzard can find a carcass, any hog a place to wallow, any butcher-bird a thorn on which to impale its victim? Why worry more about shabby clothes than worn-out opinions? Why worry about trouble that cannot come until some other time?

There is no use worrying about posterity. Let us all set a few more good examples. There is no use worrying about America's future. Let us live right and go to the polls and vote right. There is no use worrying about our health. Learn how to eat sensibly. There is no use worrying about women's styles. Let us reform masculine conduct. There is no use worrying about heresy. Let us all practice more Christianity. There is no use worrying about assaults on the Bible. Let us adorn its doctrines in all things. There is no use worrying about tomorrow. Make today the best day you have ever lived.

Well! Yes. I would find much joy in burying Worry— remembering how many have given Worry guest-room hospitality in life—and that Worry has brought many down in misery to premature graves.

Great gladness and gratitude would be mine if I could conduct the funeral of the supercilious, deceiving, dooming, damning fool.

G. Mr. Infidelity.

Yes! How I would like to bury this one—deep down. How I would like to sing over his grave. How I would get pleasure in announcing the death of this age-old fool, this licentious robber!

Today you may reach into a man's purse and steal his gold. You may reach into the ballot box and steal or misplace his vote. Today you may reach into his home and take his sons to fight wars. Today you may reach into his past and bring out old ghosts of barbaric intolerance and cruelty to plague him. Today you may dig up out of its grave some old scandal, and about all these things many men raise more fuss than they do when someone comes along and takes away their God.

Consider the unbelief that is *belief*. "But I have no faith," says the infidel. He deceives himself. He lies. Don't you know it takes faith to be an atheist, to be an infidel? A man cannot believe without believing that he believes. And a man cannot disbelieve without believing that he disbelieves. The atheist must believe that Providence is an idle dream. The atheist must believe that prayer is a useless exercise. The atheist must believe that heaven is a vain hope. The atheist must believe that life is without inspiration. The atheist must believe that death is without anticipation. The atheist must believe that sorrow is without balm. The atheist must believe that conscience is without authority. The atheist must believe that sin is without accountability. That is the belief of the infidel's unbelief.

Blush, you infidel, because of such belief of unbelief. Hush, if you feel the least inclination to open your mouth and defend such an idiotic position. If any newspaper is published in heaven, the belief of your unbelief will appear in the comic strip.

Infidelity and atheism and agnosticism will not do to live by. They will not do to die by. They offer wax swords for the conflicts of life. They offer painted fire for the wintry season of life. They offer painted water for the thirsts of life. They offer paper boats for the whirling rapids and dread abysses we have to dare in life. And all accurately argued sophistries of human imagination fail when brought to the great realities of death and of the great hereafter.

Infidelity fails when the shadows gather and the darkness falls. Infidelity and atheism have no provision for the "swelling Jordan." Infidelity has no staff upon which to lean when human strength fails. Infidelity has no eyes in the valley of the shadow of death. Infidelity has no lamp for a dark place.

God pity those who trust not in the *living, loving God*. Let us not forget that God abhors the sin of unbelief. The holy angels in heaven abhor it. And of this awful, appalling and base sin some of you to whom I talk may be guilty.

Don't rest another day under such awful guilt.

He that believeth on him is not condemned: but he that believeth not is condemned already, because he hath not believed in the name of the only begotten Son of God. . . . He that believeth on the Son hath everlasting life: and he that believeth not the Son shall not see life; but the wrath of God abideth on him (John 3:18, 36).

Live not and die not with the wrath of God abiding on you.

5 The Two Thieves

And with him they crucify two thieves; the one on his right hand, and the other on his left. And the scripture was fulfilled, which saith, And he was numbered with the transgressors (Mark 15:27–28).

Call the two who were crucified with him *robbers*. Or call them *thieves*. Both are *malefactors*. Some travelers, no doubt, could testify that by these they had been robbed on the highways of the land. Some home owners, too, could say that by these their houses had been ransacked. Some could assuredly say that by these their lives had been threatened. Many dark nights, with multitudinous tongues, "like the whispering leaves of a wind-stirred oak," could speak of their burglaries. Many bypaths, had they but tongues to talk, could have testified of their dastardly depredations. And these two malefactors, their minds once active in planning crimes, their hearts black with evil, their hands stained with human blood, were crucified with Jesus—to put the same brand upon Jesus. Maybe they, these two evil men, were Jewish fanatics who made insurrection against the Roman power, and used this as a pretext for rapine and murder. And with these malefactors, with the intention to give the people an impression that Jesus was to be classed with them, and probably with the purpose to take away the imputation of having punished an innocent man, Jesus was crucified. And thus was fulfilled the prophecy of Isaiah, which reads now, since the crucifixion, more like history than prophecy:

Therefore will I divide him a portion with the great, and he shall divide the spoil with the strong; because he hath poured out his soul unto death: and he was numbered with the transgressors; and he bare the sin of many, and made intercession for the transgressors (Isaiah 53:12).
And the scripture was fulfilled which saith, And he was numbered with the transgressors (Mark 15:28).

And today we now know and believe that Christ, loved by God before the foundation of the world, was "numbered with the transgressors" on Calvary's dark and bloody hill where, "noisy as burial howlers at full cry," "the people . . . and the rulers also with them derided him"—scoffed at Him, an unruly, turbulent, shouting, scoffing, mocking crowd, as void of pity as "a maniac drummer in mid-battle," a crowd bellowing as does the sea in a tempest, shrieking "like laughter in the demoned hills." And some "fierce as Frenzy's furious blood," said: "He saved others! Let him save himself!" This, of course, He could do if He were Christ, the Messiah. They implied that Christ was a cheat, a mere trickster, who had deceived the people, unless He proved His power by using it to save Himself from crucifixion. But He did not come down from the cross. He remained there, while every breath He drew was a torture, while every beat of His heart was cruel pain, in order that He might save others. They imagined that if Christ would do as they proposed they would believe on Him. But they would not have believed. They would have found some other excuse for not believing. For He did something more wonderful than they now asked. He rose from the grave. Yet they did not believe.

And shall we be ashamed of Jesus because He was "numbered with the transgressors"? Shall we blush to own His name because He who numbereth the stars and calleth them by name refused to leave His cross between two thieves? Shall we refuse or fail to give allegiance to Him who bore our sins in his own body on the tree and became for us—on the cross—all that God must judge that we through faith in Him might become all that God cannot judge? God forbid. Listen lovingly to Lorimer: "The Roman would not deny his allegiance to the imperial eagle which he defended, and in our day it would be regarded as baseness for a man to repudiate the mother who bore him, the country that sheltered him, or the college that educated him." Much more base is it for a soul to reject Jesus as Saviour, as Prophet, as Priest, as King, and as Lord, in whom is "a glory greater than ever circled the ancient seven-hilled city,"—from whom all of us have received favors which excel in grandeur all that parents, all that country, all that schools can confer. How we label ourselves as cheap and sordid and sinful when, and if, we are ashamed of Jesus.

> Ashamed of Jesus! Sooner far
> May evening blush to own a star. . . .
> Ashamed of Jesus! Just as soon
> Might midnight blush to think of noon.
> 'Twas midnight with my soul till He,
> Bright Morning Star, bade darkness flee.

"Two thieves"—who had cast away in Folly's court and Carnal Pleasure's mart, the wealth God gave them at the start, in the opportunities of life. "And Jesus in the midst."

"Two thieves"—who, by evil-doing had set, with their own wicked hands, the crown of infamy upon their own brows.

"And Jesus in the midst"—a spotless and innocent lamb between two snarling wolves.

"Two thieves"—the air hideous all around with invective, hearing the coarse mockeries, "cast the same in his teeth" (Matthew 27:44).

"And Jesus in the midst"—God's nightingale, with voice of love, between two puff adders with venom in their voices.

Amid the darkness, and louder than the crash of rocks loosened by earthquake, there were those concerning whom this was true:

And they that passed by railed on him, wagging their heads, and saying, Ah, thou that destroyest the temple, and buildest it in three days, Save thyself, and come down from the cross (Mark 15:29-30).

And of the chief priests it is written:

Likewise also the chief priests mocking said among themselves with the scribes, He saved others; himself he cannot save. Let Christ the King of Israel descend now from the cross, that we may see and believe . . . (Mark 15:31-32).

"And Jesus in the midst"—holy recipient of their foul abuse.

"Two thieves"—any beautiful dreams they had ever had now molded in the muck and mud and mess of their transgressions—standing on the border line of eternity, reviling Him whom all the angels of God worship.

"And Jesus in the midst"—Rose of Sharon between two cactus plants.

"Two thieves"—all their years eaten by the locusts of evil, yawning pits of black despair before them.

"And Jesus in the midst"—a dove between two hissing serpents.

And one thief said:

And one of the malefactors which were hanged railed on him, saying, "If thou be Christ, save thyself and us (Luke 23:39).

Talmage says of this:

"If thou be the Son of God." Was there any "if" about it? Tell me, thou star that in robe of light did run to point out His birthplace. Tell me, thou sea that didst put thy hand over thy lip when He bade thee be still. Tell me, thou sun in mid-heaven, who for Him didst pull down over thy face the veil of darkness. Tell me, ye lepers who were cleansed, ye dead who were raised, is He the Son of God? Aye! Aye! responds the universe. The flowers breathe it; the stars chime it; the redeemed celebrate it; the angels rise on their thrones to announce it. And yet on that miserable malefactor's "if" how many shall be wrecked for all eternity? That little "if" has enough venom in its sting to cause the death of a soul. No "if" about it. I know it. *Ecce Deus!* I feel it thoroughly—through every muscle of the body and through every faculty of my mind and through every energy of my soul. Living I will preach it; dying, I will pillow my head upon its consolations—Jesus, the God.

But, somehow, during these wild and wicked scenes, one thief had quickly and surely grown penitent. "As men who have been nearly drowned tell us that in one moment while they were under the water their whole life passed before them, so I suppose in one moment the dying malefactor thought over all his past life." He looked upon himself as a guilty wretch, as one who deserved to die. In that time of torment, he saw the sin and futility of blaspheming Christ who had done him no wrong. Yet the malefactor felt he could not die as he had lived, in sin and rebellion against God. The tortures of his guilty soul becoming more painful than the tortures of his body, he saw his past as a scene of misdoing, saw himself as guilty of "the mightiest felony in the universe," for he had robbed God, had robbed God of his time and of his talent, robbed Him of his service. And so, he spoke, answering the reviling and still impenitent comrade in crime:

Dost not thou fear God, seeing thou art in the same condemnation? And we indeed justly; for we receive the due reward of our deeds: but this man hath done nothing amiss (Luke 23:40–41).

And that dying, penitent thief, at the moment, saw Jesus as the friend of the outcast. He saw Jesus as the Lamb of God giving His life as a ransom for many! He saw Jesus as the One sent from God—to die. He saw Jesus as One who, in life, in death, proved that God's unfathomed love is greater than man's sin and folly—in life, in death, proved that there is a wideness in God's mercy like the wideness of the sea. Yea, though the thief saw late, yet at last he saw.

This dying thief, looked upon by the crucifiers as merely dying vermin, looked upon as despicable dust which no man values, the ruined pivots and pulleys of his rending physical mechanism falling apart, maybe in his mind and heart a far-off vision of the Lake of Galilee and quiet hills and a home of peace whose threshold he shall cross no more, desires to fall asleep on some kind bosom. So, gazing upon the face of Christ, through the thickening gloom, he calls unto him somewhat as a wounded animal caught in the jaws of a steel trap wailingly appeals for help. He said: ". . . Lord, remember me when thou comest into thy kingdom" (Luke 23:42).

And as he spoke in praise, amid the mockings and jeers of the mob, his was the one voice which attested Him Redeemer when all had forsaken Him and fled. His was the tortured voice which was the one note of sweetness in the wild, unmusical discord. His was the voice, though the voice of a malefactor, for whose evil deeds there is neither apology nor defense, which was the one cry of faith in the hour of infinite denial and rejection. So now we hear the impenitent thief railing, like a hissing adder dying in the fire. And we hear the penitent thief rebuking and praying.

One of the thieves dying in despair. The other coming out of his bondage, sorrow, and night into Christ's freedom, gladness and light. One choosing the way that leads to night and the dark dungeons of hell. The other choosing the road that leads to light and the mansions eternal in the heavens. One going to deeper depths of ruin untold. The other coming out from the depths into the peace of God's sheltering fold. What a picture we have here of men today, some of whom choose the way of destruction, some of whom choose the way of eternal life. Some choose the deserts of a growing and eternal wasting, some the blossoming fields of God's paradise. Some, living in the same place where others are saved, choose the place where men and women are "burning continually, yet unconsumed; forever wasting, yet enduring still; dying perpetually, yet never dead." But some, like the thief who cried for mercy, choose the place where death's shadows and sin's slime and sorrow's sighs are never known. Some, unlike the railing thief, choose with the rebuking thief, choose a throne where with Christ they shall sit and reign.

A thief—a penitent thief. Nothing behind him but the ashes of a wasted life; nothing before but the fires of an eternal hell! Nothing behind but the folly of a sinful life; nothing ahead but the horrors of a sinner's death. Nothing behind but blight;

nothing ahead but night—the awful outer darkness! Nothing behind but error; nothing before but terror! Nothing behind but gloom; nothing ahead but doom! No angels of consolation will speak his name when he goes shuddering through the gates of death. Dark, very dark, it will be there. Dreadful, dreadfully dreadful, it will be there. Lonely, terribly lonely, it will be there. So he puts all his tangled thoughts into one prayer: "Lord, remember me when thou comest into thy kingdom!" The cry is that of an utterly friendless man, a man to whom the loneliness of death is a most tremendous terror. Yet this thief, seeing Him as Saviour, cried out from the depths of a vast abyss: "Lord, remember me when thou comest into thy kingdom!"

But there is another there whose hidden glory bursts through the dark cloud that veiled it. Jesus—able, willing, mighty to save! Jesus—bearing our sins in his own body on the tree! Jesus! He refused the invitation of the mob to come down from the cross to prove His divinity. And out of the depths of an infinite love, which no waters can drown, no fires consume, no blizzards freeze, He reaches out to the rescue of the dying thief! Christ Jesus will enter the other world with this poor dying thief upon His bosom. Shall friend or angel of judgment claim this man's soul when it is Christ who justifies? Nay! Nay! Never! For the thief saw him, hailed him as King—as Saviour. Great faith that—blossoming like a lily in a desert! Wonderful faith that—shining amid the world's unbelief like a sun at midnight! Marvelous faith that—giving forth fragrance like a full-blown rose in a garbage lot!

And so there were three crosses and three who died there that day on Calvary.

One died *for* sin. That was Jesus.

One died *in* sin. That one was the impenitent thief.

One died saved *from* sin. That one was the penitent thief.
One died in *love*. That one was Jesus.
One died in *despair*. That one was the impenitent thief.
One died in *faith*. That one was the penitent thief.
One died a Benefactor. That one was Jesus.
One died a blasphemer. That one was the impenitent thief.
One died a believer. That one was the penitent thief.

There were three trees planted in a row that day. And all three bore fruit. One tree yielded poison—the tree on which the impenitent malefactor died. One tree yielded bitter aloes—aloes "bitter as coloquintida"—the tree on which the penitent thief died, "his heart within burnt like an aftertaste of sin to one whose memory drinks and loathes the lee of shame and sorrow deeper than the sea." One tree—the middle tree—bore the beautiful apples of love. That was the tree on which Jesus died. "Norway pine and tropical orange and Lebanon cedar would not make so strange a grove as this orchard of Calvary."

One tree yielded blossoms. That was the tree on which the penitent thief gasped his last breath. One tree yielded briars. That was the tree where the wretched criminal, holding in his face the sorrow of that unblessed hour, "turning around on his spikes to hiss at Jesus"—Jesus whose name sounds down the corridors of the centuries like the music of all choirs, visible and invisible, poured forth in one anthem. One tree yielded blood—blood "drawn from Immanuel's veins." And that, of course, was the tree on which Jesus died. One tree was the tree of rejection—the impenitent's tree. One tree was the tree of reception—the penitent's tree. One tree was the tree of redemption—the Saviour's tree.

Let us close with some words of Talmage in our ears and hearts:

"I have shown you the right-hand cross and the left-hand cross. Now come to the middle cross. We have stood at the one and found it yielded poison. We have stood at the other and found it yielded bitter aloes. Come now to the middle cross, and shake down apples of love. Uncover your head. You never saw so tender a scene as this. You may have seen father and mother die, or companion or child die, but never so affecting a scene as this. The railing thief looked from one way and saw only the right side of Christ's face. The penitent thief looked from the other way and saw the left side of Christ's face. But in the full blaze of gospel light you see Christ's full face. It was a suffering face. Human hate had done its worst and hell had hurled its sharpest javelin —and devils had vented their hottest rage, when, with every nerve in His body in torture and every fibre of His heart in excruciation, He died.

To the middle cross look, that your souls may live. I showed you the right-hand cross in order that you might see what an awful thing it is to be unbelieving. I showed you the left-hand cross that you might see what it is to repent. Now I shall show you the middle cross that you may see what Christ has done to save your soul. Poets have sung its praise, sculptors have attempted to commemorate it in marble. Martyrs have clung to it in fire, and Christians, dying quietly in their beds, have leaned their heads against it. This hour may all our souls embrace it with an ecstasy of affection. Lay hold of that cross! Put your hand on that and you are safe, though the world swings beneath your feet.

Throw down at the foot of that middle cross sin, sorrow, life, death—everything. We are slaves; Christ gives deliverance to the captive. We are thirsty; Christ is the river of salvation to slake our thirst. We are hungry; Jesus says: "I am the bread of life." We are condemned to die; Christ says: "Save that man from going down into the pit; I am the ransom." We are tossed on the sea of trouble; Jesus comes over it, saying: "It is I. Be not afraid!" We are in darkness; Jesus says: "I am the Bright and Morning Star!" We are sick; Jesus is the "Balm of Gilead." We are dead; hear the shrouds rend and the grave hillocks heave as He cried: "I am the rescurrection and the life; he that believeth in me though he were dead, yet shall he live." We want justification; "Being justified by faith we have peace with God through our Lord Jesus Christ." We want to exercise faith: "Believe in the Lord Jesus Christ, and thou shalt be saved." I want to get from under condemnation; "There is now therefore no condemnation to them who are in Christ Jesus."

> The dying thief rejoiced to see
> That fountain in his day;
> And there may I, though vile as he,
> Wash all my sins away;
> Wash all my sins away,
> Wash all my sins away;
> And there may I, though vile as he,
> Wash all my sins away.

6 The Theology of the Penitent Thief

And when they were come to the place, which is called Calvary, there they crucified him, and the malefactors, one on the right hand, and the other on the left (Luke 23:33).

We hear much talk today of Karl Barth's theology, of Calvin's theology, of Luther's theology, of Augustine's theology, of Strong's theology, and of the theology of many others who claim to be able to speak of God and to expound the Word of God. What is theology? It is, according to Webster's dictionary, "the science that treats of the existence, nature, and attributes of God, especially of man's relations to God, knowledge of God and the supernatural." "A thief" is defined as one who steals, one who takes unlawfully what is not his own. Then to speak of the theology of a thief seems like putting poison ivy and roses together for a bouquet, mud and soap together for the washing of dishes, vinegar and sugar together for the sweetening of coffee, idiocy and intelligence in one skull for scholarship, soot and snow together in the same cleansing mixture.

We hear of schools of theology, and many theologians, some magnificent, some mediocre. We have the Southern Baptist Seminary in Louisville, the New Orleans Baptist Theological Seminary in Louisiana, the Southwestern Baptist Theological Seminary, in Fort Worth, the Southeastern Theological Seminary, in North Carolina, the Golden Gate Theological Seminary, in California, and the Dallas Theological Seminary in Texas. And many other theological schools in other cities of the world.

As to theology, there are many and divergent views held by men of different times and places.

There was Arminius who declared that he meant to break down all orthodox creeds and reduce all Christians to the level of one common rationalistic religion. There was Arius who taught that God has not always been Father, that Jesus is not from Eternity, that Jesus came from nothing. There was Athanasius who taught that God and Jesus and the Holy Spirit are equal in power and glory, through all the bitterness and rage of partisanship, even though the church and the world combined against him. To him we owe under God the entire power of modern evangelical Christianity.

But I speak now of the theology of a thief, a penitent thief— yea, of a thief naked and dying beside Jesus Christ, himself the victim of excesses of savage malice, on a Roman cross. This thief, confessing that he deserved the death meted out to him, with nothing behind but gloom and nothing ahead but doom, with nothing but a way of error behind and nothing but a way of terror ahead, with nothing but the ashes of a misspent life behind and nothing but the eternal fires of hell ahead, with nothing but a life of blight in the past and nothing but eternal night in the future, gave forth, though he knew it not, a theology men need to have and to hold today. That theology was not set forth from some classroom, but with Calvary's bloody hill as the place and a bloodied wooden cross as a pulpit.

What a day for this thieving criminal. In the sun-kissed dawn: sentenced to crucifixion. In the bright morning: shackled in Pilate's dungeon. At the darkened noonday: in torment on a cross. At sundown: in the beauty and peace of Paradise.

We read that when they brought Jesus out for crucifixion, they brought out two robbers under condemnation for their crimes.

> Then delivered he him therefore unto them to be crucified. And they took Jesus, and led him away. And he bearing his cross went forth into a place called the place of a skull, which is called in the Hebrew Golgotha: Where they crucified him, and two other with him, on either side one, and Jesus in the midst (John 19:16–18).

On the way to Calvary's hill, each one condemned to crucifixion wore a placard fixed on the back, according to the custom, describing the crime. On the backs of the two thieves the placard read "robber and murderer." On Jesus' scourge-cut back the placard read "King of the Jews." These were the same words which composed the superscription which was written over Jesus in letters of Greek, and Latin, and Hebrew (Luke 23:38).

> And Pilate wrote a title, and put it on the cross. And the writing was, Jesus of Nazareth the King of the Jews (John 19:19).

When the scribes and Pharisees saw Jesus, their chief enemy, spiked to and uplifted on the cross, a shout of joy and derision went up from them. A whirlpool of blasphemy and execration raged like a maelstrom about the cross. Behold human nature reaching the climax of its infamy and shame! Listen to the mockers!

"Ah! You were going to destroy the temple, and build it again in three days, were you? What about that now? You said you were the Son of God. If you are, where now is your God? Why does he let you hang here on a cross?"

"You saved others! Why can't you save yourself?"

"You are a king, are you? But if so, where is your crown, for we see nothing but a crown of thorns. Where is your royal robe? We see only the crimson robe of your blood."

"They said you worked miracles! Then give us another miracle! They say you raised Lazarus from the dead, and the daughter of Jairus and the widow's son at Nain. How about another miracle now—and so save yourself from death? You healed the paralytic and the leper, and cast the devils out of the Gadarene. Now can't you do something for yourself? Give us just one more miracle. Come down from the cross—and we will believe on you."

The two thieves, companions in crime, "cast the same in his teeth" (Matthew 27:44)—with lips curling in sneers while they twitched with pain.

"You are indeed a King! Then prove it. Prove that your head merits a crown. Prove that your hand has the right to wield a sceptre. Come down from that cross. Take us down, too! Set up your throne. And we two thieves will be your prime ministers. And what a kingdom that will be!" In words like these they spoke.

For a period of time both thieves were taunting and cursing Jesus, like adders spitting venom.

But suddenly one of them becomes strangely silent. After a little he breaks the silence with no hesitant words, rebukes his companion in crime, who had said to Jesus, "If thou be Christ, save thyself and us" (Luke 23:39).

But the other answering rebuked him, saying, Dost not thou fear God, seeing thou art in the same condemnation? And we indeed justly; for we receive the due reward of our deeds: but this man hath done nothing amiss (Luke 23:40, 41).

Then, while torments traveled every artery and vein of his body, he turns his head toward Jesus and, in agonizing desperation, makes a request—with lips parched and with tongue hot with the drouth of blood—asking: "And he said unto Jesus, Lord, remember me when thou comest into thy kingdom" (Luke 23:42).

With the flame of joy which was in his heart lighting up his drawn and blood-streaked face, Jesus answered, "Verily I say unto thee, To day shalt thou be with me in paradise" (Luke 23:43).

Thus did Jesus prove that He is able to save to the uttermost (Hebrews 7:25).

As one wrote, if we search the Bible through from Genesis to Revelation, we shall never find a more striking proof of Christ's power and mercy than the salvation of the penitent thief.

Look at the three crosses on the place of a skull. One was the cross of *atonement*—the cross on which Jesus died. One was the cross of *abhorrence*—the cross on which the impenitent thief died. One was the cross of *acceptance*—the cross on which the penitent thief died.

And let us think of the theology of that penitent thief who, without character, without baptism, without any good works to boast about, with nothing in his past life to commend him, was saved by God's unmerited favor to the utterly undeserving. Yes, saved *suddenly* with no mysterious delay, no purgatory, "between his death and a state of reward." In the day he draws his last painful breath he goes to Paradise. In the hour he departs he is with Christ (Philippians 1:23).

Let us think with thoughtful concentration of the theology of this thief who died a believer.

Note first that he believed that:

I. ETERNAL THINGS MATTER MOST.

This saved thief said to his companion in crime: "Dost thou not fear God?"

God was the eternal One whom he feared.

The other thief, in dark impenitence, was fearing man. Today we should be little concerned about what *men* think of us and say about us. But we should be much concerned about what *God* knows about us. We should prove by holy living that the sober truth of Job's words has influenced our lives.

For the ear trieth words, as the mouth tasteth meat. Let us choose to us judgment: let us know among ourselves what is good. For Job hath said, I am righteous: and God hath taken away my judgment. Should I lie against my right? my wound is incurable without transgression. What man is like Job, who drinketh up scorning like water? (Job 34:3–7).

Remembering that it is impossible to flee from God's presence, we should never forget these words of the psalmist:

If I say, Surely the darkness shall cover me; even the night shall be light about me. Yea, the darkness hideth not from thee; but the night shineth as the day: the darkness and the light are both alike to thee (Psalm 139:11–12).

We should remember what God said to Samuel, who was looking favorably upon Eliab, son of Jesse, for the kingship:

But the Lord said unto Samuel, Look not on his countenance, or on the height of his stature; because I have refused him: for the Lord seeth not as man seeth; for man looketh on the outward appearance, but the Lord looketh on the heart (I Samuel 16:7).

What matters most is not man's applause but God's approval —not man pleasing man but man pleasing God.

Remembering that even Christ pleased not Himself (Romans 15:3), we should so live that what was written of Enoch could and would be known of us: ". . . for before his translation he had this testimony, that he pleased God" (Hebrews 11:5).

This truth is proved in the theology of the penitent thief.

Again, the dying criminal believed that:

II. HE WAS A SINNER.

He spoke of "the same condemnation" (Luke 23:40). He said to his dying criminal companion: "And we indeed justly; for we receive the due reward of our deeds . . ." (Luke 23:41). This thief's theology included the truth that the thorns we reap are of our own planting, that the bitter water the sinner drinks is from the well of his own digging and from fountains he himself opens. The thief knew that the fires that scorch the sinner are of his own kindling, that the ditch in which he found himself inextricably engulfed was of his own digging.

All men everywhere have to confess this truth: "For all have sinned, and come short of the glory of God" (Romans 3:23).

King Pharaoh, who lived as though he had been nursed on the tiger milk of cruelty, said: "I have sinned." Achan, greedy for gold and garments, said: "I have sinned." King Saul, his heart stubborn and in rebellion against the will of God, said:

"I have sinned." David, staking his crown for a woman's caress, said, in contrition: "I have sinned."

The Prodigal, back from the hog trough, said to his father: "I have sinned." Judas Iscariot, ridden with the devils of remorse, throwing down the thirty pieces of silver as though they were hissing serpents or burning coals of fire, said: "I have sinned." Peter, after a fruitless night of fishing, saw two ships filled to the sinking point with fishes, and we read: "I am a sinful man, O Lord." Paul spoke of himself as the chief of sinners (I Timothy 1:15).

So must we all confess that we are grievous sinners.

We note that the theology of the dying thief holds the truth that he believed:

III. HE COULD BE SAVED.

Note the mockeries of the mob around the cross, the mocking and reviling words of "the chief priests, the scribes, the elders":

He saved others; himself he cannot save. If he be the King of Israel, let him now come down from the cross, and we will believe him. He trusted in God; let him deliver him now, if he will have him: for he said, I am the Son of God" (Matthew 27:42–43).

Let Christ the King of Israel descend now from the cross, that we may see and believe. And they that were crucified with him reviled him (Mark 15:32).

But this dying thief believed he could be rescued from the pit he had digged for himself. He believed that he could be taken from the plight and place of condemnation to the peace and place of coronation.

He believed that, evil as he was, he could go from this condition to which crime had brought him to heavenly companionship, from night to day, from bondage to liberty.

And he believed that he could be saved without any character to mention; and he believed he could be saved without baptism—for he had no chance to be baptized, even if there were such a thing as salvation by baptism. He believed he could be saved without any record of good works. And in this the Apostle Paul, who compassed the earth with the truths of redemption, is in agreement, for we read:

That in the ages to come he might shew the exceeding riches of his grace in his kindness toward us through Christ Jesus. For by grace are ye saved through faith; and that not of yourselves: it is the gift of God: Not of works, lest any man should boast (Ephesians 2:7–9).

Somehow he glimpsed the truth that sin is stain, and divine forgiveness the bath which cleanses it away. Somehow he had gotten hold of the truth that sin is the blotted and blurred page and divine forgiveness the erasure of the page. Somehow he knew now that sin is darkness, and divine forgiveness the light which dispels it. Somehow he knew that blessed would he be if his transgressions were forgotten, his sins forgiven.

Then, too, the theology of the dying thief shows that he believed in:

IV. RETRIBUTION FOR THE WICKED.

He said: "We receive the due rewards of our deeds." He believed that 'tis just for a man to reap what he sows. He believed that when a man sows the wind, he can expect to reap the whirlwind, that the man who digs a ditch for another should have no complaint if he himself falls in that ditch and finds it his grave. He believed that a man who rolls a stone upon another should show no surprise if the stone returns upon himself with crushing weight in increase. Winston Churchill had that thief's theology when he said: "The lashes Italy now receives are from the whips she put upon Ethiopia's back."

He knew the truth Paul later expressed: "Be not deceived; God is not mocked: for whatsoever a man soweth, that shall he also reap" (Galatians 6:7).

And we need to remember these words from the poets:

> Remember Milo's end,
> Wedged in that timber which he strove to rend.

and

Though the mills of God grind slowly, yet they grind exceeding small.

In so many ways in personal, domestic, and national life do we find that the man who sows the wind of vanity shall reap the whirlwind of wrath. A man is a fool to think he can evade the laws of nature and mock nature's God. Yet equally foolish is he who sows wickedness and expects to reap safety at last. Retribution trails down those who violate the laws of God.

Moreover, we learn something of the dying thief's theology when we learn that he believed in:

V. HIS OWN INABILITY TO SAVE HIMSELF.

His hands were spiked to the cross. His feet were spiked to the cross. He could do nothing to lessen his pain. He could do nothing to pull out the nails from hands and feet. He could do nothing to keep his ears from hearing the expressions of rage of the hooting mob. So we need that theology ourselves. We need to know that "not by works of righteousness we have done" can we be saved. We need to know that:

Could our zeal no respite know,
Could our tears forever flow,
All for sin could not atone,
Christ must save and Christ alone.

Naaman could not cure himself of his leprosy. And at first he went into a foolish rage over the place the prophet prescribed for his cure. We read:

So Naaman came with his horses and with his chariot, and stood at the door of the house of Elisha. And Elisha sent a messenger unto him, saying, Go and wash in Jordan seven times, and thy flesh shall come again to thee, and thou shalt be clean. But Naaman was wroth, and went away, and said, Behold, I thought, He will surely come out to me, and stand, and call on the name of the Lord his God, and strike his hand over the place, and recover the leper. Are not Abana and Pharpar, rivers of Damascus, better than all the waters of Israel? may I not wash in them, and be clean? So he turned and went away in a rage (II Kings 5:9–12).

But Naaman was cured by God's plan, not his. God *could* cure. And God *did* cure.

We need to preach and sing in glad and grateful reiteration the words: "What can wash away my sin? Nothing but the blood of Jesus."

Listen to God's Word:

For though thou wash thee with nitre, and take thee much sope, yet thine iniquity is marked before me, saith the Lord God (Jeremiah 2:22).

Can the Ethiopian change his skin, or the leopard his spots? then may ye also do good, that are accustomed to do evil (Jeremiah 13:23).

And rejoice in this:

Come now, and let us reason together, saith the Lord: though your sins be as scarlet, they shall be as white as snow; though they be red like crimson, they shall be as wool (Isaiah 1:18).

Christina Rossetti wrote, in "The Battle Within":

> God harden me against myself,
> The coward with pathetic voice
> Who craves for ease, and rest, and joys:
>
> Myself, arch-traitor to myself;
> My hollowest friend, my deadliest foe,
> My clog whatever road I go.
>
> Yet One there is can curb myself,
> Can roll the strangling load from me,
> Break off the yoke and set me free.

And Paul wrote: "For the law of the Spirit of life in Christ Jesus hath made me free from the law of sin and death" (Romans 8:2). Blessed freedom!

Again, the dying thief believed that:

VI. SALVATION MUST BE ENTIRELY OF GRACE.

In that he was a wiser theologian than many who claim to be theologians today. "Remember me," he said. "Remember me"—not because I deserve remembrance, not because I merit mercy, not because I am good, not because I've helped others, not because I am a man of honor, not because I've broken no commandments.

But because, and *all* because, and *only* because, of God's unlimited and unmerited favor to the utterly undeserving. By that matchless and marvelous grace of God was the thief saved, even as are all who are saved.

For by grace are ye saved through faith; and that not of your-selves: it is the gift of God: Not of works, lest any man should boast (Ephesians 2:8–9).

Being justified freely by his grace through the redemption that is in Christ Jesus: Whom God hath set forth to be a propitiation through faith in his blood, to declare his righteousness for the re-mission of sins that are past, through the forbearance of God (Romans 3:24–25).

For the grace of God that bringeth salvation hath appeared to all men (Titus 2:11).

And being beneficiaries of this matchless and manifold grace of God (I Peter 4:10), we should hold in mind these words:

Teaching us that, denying ungodliness and worldy lusts, we should live soberly, righteously, and godly, in this present world; Looking for that blessed hope and the glorious appearing of the great God and our Saviour Jesus Christ; Who gave himself for us, that he might redeem us from all iniquity, and purify unto himself a peculiar people, zealous of good works (Titus 2:12–14).

Giving thought to the dying thief's theology, we learn that he believed in:

VII. THE SINLESSNESS OF CHRIST JESUS.

". . . this man hath done nothing amiss" (Luke 23:41).
Though he had not heard Jesus ask the question, he could answer correctly with a "nobody" Jesus' question found in John 8:46: "Which of you convinceth me of sin? And if I say the truth, why do ye not believe me?" Paul later wrote the truth that this dying thief believed—speaking of Jesus as the one who knew no sin (II Corinthians 5:21).

And in the letter to the Hebrews, we read:

For we have not an high priest which cannot be touched with the feeling of our infirmities; but was in all points tempted like as we are, yet without sin (Hebrews 4:15).

And, later on, Peter wrote words that were in agreement with what the thief said: "Who did no sin, neither was guile found in his mouth" (I Peter 2:22).

Absolutely sinless was the Christ on whose brow flashed the diadems of world creation, whose hand swayed the scepter of universal authority, whose majesty filled heaven with glory, whose wrath filled hell with terror, whose goodness filled this earth with blessing. From His cold welcome into the world on a pallet of straw until the time when He was cruelly thrust out on the point of a spear until now, no one has ever found Him guilty of breaking one of Gods' laws—in thought, in word, in deed. His life was a flawless mirror of stainless purity, reflecting the wisdom of God. As one said, Jesus is the sun on which all the telescopes of time have failed to find a flaw.

The incomparable character of Jesus Christ still shines as earth's purest diamond. He illustrated in His daily life every doctrine of His heavenly mind.

Not only so. The thief's theology sets forth:

VIII. THE DEITY OF JESUS.

"Dost thou not fear God?" the thief asked.

And, addressing Jesus, he called Him "Lord."

Nobody called Him Lord on the day when it seemed that the kingdom about which He had spoken was shrinking to the narrow dimensions of a tomb, when it seemed the only scepter He would wield was the weed placed in His hand in mockery, when it seemed His only king's cup was the sponge filled with vinegar and gall, when it seemed that all the hopes of His disciples were dying with the naked body of their Master on the cross.

"Lord" means one having supreme power and authority. Some people have not called Him "Lord" in spite of the fact of His world-wide influence for nineteen centuries.

Peter called him "Lord" after he had witnessed the great draught of fishes. Thomas called Him "Lord" after he had felt the wounds in His side. Paul called him "Lord" after he had had a glorious vision of Him.

But what a faith this dying thief had—faith blossoming like a lily in a butcher's slaughter pen—when he called Jesus "Lord" as he saw Him dying on a cross.

In his dying agonies, the thief reasoned that the life that had "nothing amiss" in it demanded deity as explanation. Jesus was the verity of God's truth; Jesus was the beauty of God's holiness; Jesus was the purity of God's nature; Jesus was the reality of God's love; Jesus was the surety of God's promise; Jesus was the majesty of God's power; Jesus was the authority of God's throne; Jesus was the pity of God's heart; Jesus was the repository of God's fullness; Jesus was the legacy of God's will; Jesus was the ocean of all God's full and flowing rivers of grace.

The dying thief believed that Jesus was Lord—"very God of very God." Again, this dying thief believed that Jesus was:

IX. HEAVEN'S KING.

This dying criminal recognized Jesus was *the* king, though He had no throne but a cross, no crown but a crown of thorns, no scepter but nails in His hands, no royal wardrobe but shameful nakedness.

The hissing mob said: "We have no king but Caesar!" In substance they said: "A king? Then a crown he must have." So they crowned Him with a crown of thorns. "A king? Then the insignia of his high office he needs." So, with the merciless knout, they seamed His quivering flesh until it started up in red scars. "A king? Then we must give testimony of our allegiance." So they spat into His face. "A king? Then we must raise and reach our hands to him!" So they beat Him with their fists, slapped Him with hard palms, pulled out His beard. "A king? Then regal robes he must wear." So they, with a studied indignity, put on Him a purple robe. "A king? Then a scepter he ought to have!" So they, in vulgar jest, put a reed in His hand. "A king? Then a proclamation must be made!" So they bowed the knee in jest and scoffingly said, "Hail, King of the Jews!" "A king? Then he ought to have a coronation psalm." So they, with rabble-frenzy, cried out "Crucify Him!" "A king? Then a right royal procession he must have!" So they led Him, as a lamb to the slaughter, to Golgotha. "A king? Then he ought to have a throne." So they lifted Him upon a wooden cross, Himself nailed thereon. "A king? Then he ought to have a chalice." So they gave Him a sponge filled with vinegar and gall. Mock King!

Not so the thief! He saw Jesus as the Lord who is King forever, the King of kings, the King of glory, the everlasting Ruler of rulers. Before His crucifixion, after His resurrection, many called Jesus "Lord." But only the thief called Him "Lord" as the Potentate of potentates was dying.

Socrates had the comradeship of a few loyal friends when he drank the hemlock, but none such had the King of kings when the mob laughed to see Him die. Latimer and Ridley, martyrs of old, comforted each other in the flames. But, save the thief, no mouth spoke of Christ's kingdom when, His glory seeming to be in total eclipse, He bled His sweet life away.

But darkness could not hide from the thief the truth of his belief that Jesus was God.

We should note that in the theology of the dying thief was the belief that:

X. CHRIST WAS WILLING AND ABLE TO SAVE.

"Remember me."

All the thief asked for was to be *remembered* by Jesus. It was as if he said: "I do not ask for a high place in Thy kingdom. That I know will be given to the patriarchs and prophets and the apostles. I do not ask for these places. But, Lord, when Thou comest, remember this thief, who, at the last hour repented and called upon Thee. Grant him a place in Thy kingdom—even the lowest." This thief believed what Peter later wrote:

The Lord is not slack concerning his promise, as some men count slackness; but is longsuffering to us-ward, not willing that any should perish, but that all should come to repentance (II Peter 3:9).

Wherefore he is able to save them to the uttermost that come unto God by him, seeing he ever liveth to make intercession for them (Hebrews 7:25).

Who is this that cometh from Edom, with dyed garments from Bozrah? this that is glorious in his apparel, travelling in the greatness of his strength? I that speak in righteousness, mighty to save (Isaiah 63:1).

Now let us remember that the dying thief believed in:

XI. CHRIST'S SUBSTITUTIONARY SACRIFICE.

He said about Jesus: "The same condemnation." He said about Jesus: "He has done nothing amiss."

Note the following:

Now at that feast he released unto them one prisoner, whomsoever they desired. And there was one named Barabbas, which lay bound with them that had made insurrection with them, who had committed murder in the insurrection (Mark 15:6–7).

And they had then a notable prisoner, called Barabbas. Therefore when they were gathered together, Pilate said unto them, Whom will ye that I release unto you? Barabbas, or Jesus which is called Christ? (Matthew 27:16–17).

But the chief priests and elders persuaded the multitude that they should ask Barabbas, and destroy Jesus (Matthew 27:20).

Christ occupied the cross made for Barabbas. So we must believe that Jesus took our place on the cross. We must believe this truth:

> My sins laid open to the rod
> The back which from the law was free,
> And the eternal Son of God
> Received the stripes once due to me.
> —James M. Gray

> Jesus paid it all;
> All to Him I owe.
> —Elvina M. Hall

Jesus paid our sin debt.

> By me the sponge of vinegar and gall,
> Was placed upon His tongue,
> And when derision marked His call
> I stood that mocking crowd among.
> —James M. Gray

Let it never be a trite truth—that which Isaiah wrote:

Surely he hath borne our griefs, and carried our sorrows: yet we did esteem him stricken, smitten of God, and afflicted (Isaiah 53:4).

Also, consider the following:

For I delivered unto you first of all that which I also received, how that Christ died for our sins according to the scriptures" (I Corinthians 15:3).

Who gave himself for our sins, that he might deliver us from this present evil world, according to the will of God and our Father" (Galatians 1:4).

Who his own self bare our sins in his own body on the tree, that we, being dead to sins, should live unto righteousness: by whose stripes ye were healed" (I Peter 2:24).

Moreover, this dying thief believed in:

XII. THE RESURRECTION OF CHRIST.

The thief said: "When thou comest into thy kingdom." The thief knew Jesus was to die. Yet the thief said: "When thou comest. . . ." No dead man could do that. No dead man could come into a kingdom. We must believe in the resurrection of Jesus.

Paul said:

Now if Christ be preached that he rose from the dead, how say some among you that there is no resurrection of the dead? But if there be no resurrection of the dead, then is Christ not risen: And if Christ be not risen, then is our preaching vain, and your faith is also vain. Yea, and we are found false witnesses of God; because we have testified of God that he raised up Christ: whom he raised not up, if so be that the dead rise not. For if the dead rise not, then is not Christ raised: And if Christ be not raised, your faith is vain; ye are yet in your sins. Then they also which are fallen asleep in Christ are perished. If in this life only we have hope in Christ, we are of all men most miserable (I Corinthians 15:12–19).

Finally, we get another truth from the theology of the dying thief, learning that the thief believed in:

XIII. THE FUTURE KINGDOM OF CHRIST.

"*Thy* Kingdom!"

"Thy *Kingdom!*"

There is only one way to enter this Kingdom—and Paradise. I ask David how he got in, I ask Isaiah how he got in, I ask Peter how he got in, I ask John how he got in, I ask Paul how he got in. I ask the martyrs how they got in. And all answered, "I came by the way of the penitent thief."

The Polish astronomer Copernicus was a great scientist and a great mathematician. His writings and investigations changed man's conception of the universe. When Copernicus lay dying at Franenberg, his great work, *The Revolution of the Heavenly Bodies,* just off the press, was laid in his arms. But when he came to face life's ultimate fact, and step out into the unknown, Copernicus did not think of himself as an astronomer, or a scientist, or one of the world's most learned men, but only as a sinner who put his trust in the work of Christ on the cross. On his grave you can read today the epitaph which he wrote himself:

Lord, I do not ask the kindness Thou didst show to Peter, I do not dare to ask the grace Thou didst grant to Paul; But, Lord, the mercy Thou didst show to the dying robber, that mercy show to me. That earnestly I crave.